Global Politics and Its Violent Care for Indigeneity

Marjo Lindroth • Heidi Sinevaara-Niskanen

Global Politics and Its Violent Care for Indigeneity

Sequels to Colonialism

palgrave
macmillan

Marjo Lindroth
Arctic Centre
University of Lapland
Rovaniemi, Finland

Heidi Sinevaara-Niskanen
Unit for Gender Studies
University of Lapland
Rovaniemi, Finland

ISBN 978-3-319-60981-2 ISBN 978-3-319-60982-9 (eBook)
https://doi.org/10.1007/978-3-319-60982-9

Library of Congress Control Number: 2017956206

Cover Image: © Design Pics Inc / Alamy Stock Photo
Cover Design: Akihiro Nakayama

Printed on acid-free paper

This Palgrave Macmillan imprint is published by Springer Nature
The registered company is Springer International Publishing AG
The registered company address is: Gewerbestrasse 11, 6330 Cham, Switzerland

Acknowledgments

Writing this book, and, in particular, conducting the research it is based on, has been an endeavor supported by many. Our colleagues at the University of Lapland have been of great significance in providing a research environment within which to develop our critical ideas. We wish to thank our colleagues at the Arctic Centre, Unit for Gender Studies and the Faculty of Social Sciences. A special thank you goes out to Kirsti Lempiäinen, Päivi Naskali, Julian Reid and Monica Tennberg and the Northern Political Economy research team at the Arctic Centre.

The research partners in our project Indigeneity in Waiting: Elusive Rights and the Power of Hope, funded by the Academy of Finland (2016–2020) and Kone Foundation (2016), have provided us with the invaluable fuel needed to continue to challenge our thinking. We wish to thank David Chandler, Mitchell Dean, Tanja Joona, Francesca Merlan, Frank Sejersen and Jeffrey Sissons for sharing their expertise and guidance.

The opportunity to visit several universities abroad has been vital for broadening our horizons, in terms of not only research but also gaining 'a sense of the place'. We would like to extend our warmest thanks to Australian National University and Francesca Merlan, Ilisimatusarfik/the University of Greenland and Maria Ackrén, as well as the University of Copenhagen and Frank Sejersen. Heartfelt thanks are also due to Birkbeck School of Law and Peter Fitzpatrick, Melbourne Law School and Kathleen Birrell, the University of New South Wales and Sophie Adams, as well as the University of Westminster and David Chandler.

Without the intelligence, humor and support of a number of colleagues and friends, the journey involved in writing this book would have been far less enjoyable. We would like to express our special thanks in this regard to Nina Doering, Eeva-Riitta Eerola, Richard Foley, Valeria Guerrieri, Mervi Kutuniva, Minna Nousiainen, Riikka Matala, Françoise Martz, Hanna Peltomaa, Minna Rainio, Joonas Vola and Outi Ylitapio-Mäntylä for companionship along the way. Finally, the greatest thanks are in order to families Lindroth and Sinevaara, Kaapo, Marika Lindroth and Teemu Niskanen.

Contents

CHAPTER 1

At Home in International Politics

The Promise of Progress

The origins of this book can be traced to our long journey, both individual and shared, studying indigenous peoples' position in international politics. In the course of that research, we have reflected on the meaning of progress and mustered the courage to speak out on some of the ignored or silenced issues in the prevailing political system as it invites its 'Others' to join. Originally, as scholars in international relations, we were drawn to the much-celebrated advances taken within two international political forums, the United Nations and the Arctic Council, steps that signaled greater attention to indigenous peoples' contributions and agendas. For a long time, the relations between states and indigenous peoples in international politics had remained static, with no real events signaling progress or a shift in the power positions. Now there was an air of hope and anticipation. It seemed that indigenous peoples and their situations would finally gain the political and legal attention that they deserved and that the position of the peoples in pursuing their causes had significantly improved. This being the case, the surge in indigenous peoples' engagement and inclusion in what was a relatively short time-span—from the late 1980s to the end of millennium—sparked interest and anticipation that, indeed, global politics was changing.

As we started our respective studies on the political participation of indigenous peoples in the United Nations Permanent Forum on

M. Lindroth, H. Sinevaara-Niskanen, *Global Politics and Its Violent Care for Indigeneity*,
https://doi.org/10.1007/978-3-319-60982-9_1

Indigenous Issues and the Arctic Council in the early 2000s, we were eager to reveal the dimensions of the anticipated progress. In particular, we wanted to identify the various ways in which indigenous representatives took part in these political forums and how their newly gained presence might influence the politics carried on there. At the early stages of our research, we were enthusiastic about the prospect of international politics 'moving on' and rearranging itself to be more inclusive of those whom the traditional state-based system had excluded, indigenous peoples being the premier example. The studies that we read, the people that we interviewed and the documents that we pored over were full of appreciative and congratulatory words on this moment of success in global politics. The new ethos of inclusion highlighted the novel possibilities, forms of political cooperation and leverage that the peoples had gained, a development contrasting sharply with the fact that international politics, the UN especially, had in many cases disillusioned the peoples in (not) addressing their needs. In short, our interest in politics and indigenous peoples was piqued by this period when something actually happened in global politics: indigenous peoples gained institutional access and a political platform of their own.

As years went by and piles of data accumulated, both of us in our respective research contexts became increasingly puzzled by the notion of change. It did look like some structural progress might have taken place, but in the end there was more talk about the change than a detailed analysis of the data suggested. The decision of the UN to establish the Permanent Forum on Indigenous Issues and the inclusion of indigenous representatives in the regional political cooperation in the newly established Arctic Council had opened up avenues for the peoples. However, after the eye-catching event of inviting the peoples in, very little had happened in terms of political substance, enhancing participation that was genuinely equal or taking the issues raised by indigenous representatives further. It was at this point, when both of us were struggling to articulate our critical findings, that our respective studies morphed into a joint endeavor. Over a cup of coffee, we came to realize that our respective sets of data pointed toward the same conclusion to an astonishing degree. We discovered a striking similarity in the two political spaces—Arctic politics and the UN—as regards the phrases used, the understandings of what indigenous peoples were to represent and the prevailing air of progress. From the wording of policy documents to the statements delivered, there was a tangible consensus over the significance of indigeneity and indigenous peoples' political representation in global politics. The inclusion of indigenous peoples seemed to signal an epic moment of change in politics, one giving the peoples some of the power that had previously belonged to states and genuinely valuing the peoples' knowledge, experience and worldview.

It is true that when one looks back in history, global politics and its treatment of indigenous peoples have undergone a rather significant change. It was back in the 1920s that indigenous leaders first approached the League of Nations, the predecessor of the United Nations (Indigenous Peoples' Center for Documentation, Research and Information 2017). In 1923, Chief Deskaheh, representing the Six Nations of the Iroquois, submitted a petition to the League of Nations challenging Canada's control over Iroquois lands and resources. The impetus for the petition was the violation of the peoples' rights as sovereign nations. It stated:

> We have exhausted every other recourse for gaining protection of our sovereignty by peaceful means before making this appeal to secure protection through the League of Nations. If this effort on our part shall fail we shall be compelled to resist by defensive action upon our part this British invasion of our Home-land for we are determined to live the free people that we were born. (Petition to the League of Nations, cited in Corntassel 2008, p. 110)

What the Six Nations were petitioning for was recognition of their rights, protection and just distribution of resources—the very same claims that the indigenous peoples of today pursue in and through national and global politics. Unfortunately, Chief Deskaheh was never able to take the petition to the Assembly of the League of Nations in his time, for the peoples' cause was deemed to be a domestic Canadian matter (Corntassel 2008, p. 110). In other words, indigenous issues were considered domestic concerns, and international politics was not willing, or able, to address them.

Some 80 years later, in 2002, global politics seemed to be on the verge of a new era when Kofi Annan, then Secretary-General of the United Nations, gave a speech at the first session of the recently established Permanent Forum on Indigenous Issues. Mr. Annan welcomed the indigenous representatives by saying "you have a home at the United Nations" (UN Secretary-General 2002). It looked as if international politics had taken the indigenous cause to heart; the international community seemed conscious of, and responsive to, the peoples requiring international protection and their being valid claimants for such protection. The very same politics that had previously turned its back on the peoples was now taking them under its wing. The welcoming of indigenous peoples and their issues into international politics—a forum from which they were previously explicitly excluded—has been seen as a breakthrough, a significant shift and milestone marking progress in, and of, politics.

Indeed, when it comes to indigenous peoples and international politics, there is a tendency to think that significant steps have been taken and a great deal has happened. This perception of change resonates with the idea(l) of liberal and modern politics as a politics that is assumed to be more equal, more righteous and more inclusive. Indeed, progress is the premise of liberal politics, which is thought of as improving itself and 'becoming better' (e.g. Barnett and Finnemore 2005). Plainly, the ethos of progress and promise of something better is embedded in politics, for without such an ethos, it would lose its purpose and logic. Accordingly, the inclusion of indigenous peoples and other marginalized groups has been interpreted as a signal that politics is moving forward. The extent to which progress actually takes place in politics is another question.

This book delves into global politics and the alleged change for the better in its treatment of indigenous peoples and their causes. At the core of the work is a critical discussion of power relations as well as whether, to what extent and how these relations have been (re)arranged over time. The key themes of the book, in addition to global politics and indigeneity, are contemporary colonialism, neoliberal power and the governing of life. Drawing on our individual and joint research, we argue that, despite the seemingly radical reorganization of the relations between indigenous peoples and their (previous) colonizers, what we see today is no more than the emperor's new clothes. In elaborating our argument, we undress the emperor, as it were, by scrutinizing the contemporary drive of politics to include indigenous peoples, to solicit indigenous resilience and to care for indigeneity. Our discussion reveals how, despite the current, more subtle operations of international politics, the emperor continues to rule, that is, colonial rationality prevails.

Sites for Indigeneity in International Politics

The much-touted progress in indigenous issues in global politics is not without basis. The often cited milestones in the welcoming of indigenous peoples and their issues in what has previously been the sole domain of states include fresh interest on the part of the United Nations in indigenous issues starting from the 1970s, the establishment of the UN Working Group on

Indigenous Populations in 1982, the approval of ILO Convention No. 169 concerning Indigenous and Tribal peoples in Independent Countries in 1989, the establishment of a political organization for Arctic cooperation in 1996, the forming of the UN Permanent Forum on Indigenous Issues in 2000 and the adoption of the UN Declaration on the Rights of Indigenous Peoples in 2007. These and other developments have sought to improve the peoples' abilities to be heard in international politics in order to put moral, political and legal pressure on the nation-states concerned. In addition to safeguarding the peoples' rights of political participation, the aim has been to secure their cultural, economic and social rights, on both the individual and collective levels.

At the heart of these milestones is the recognition of the continuing existence of indigenous peoples and their causes and of their role as stakeholders and claimants in global politics. In keeping with the more general transition in international relations toward a more inclusive and consultative politics, the mechanisms to include indigenous issues have relied on declaratory maneuvers that remain in the domain of soft law. The mechanisms chosen have enabled indigenous peoples to be heard and, as such, to have a footing in contemporary global politics. The UN, in particular, as a key platform for most of the events referred to as milestones, has had major significance for the global indigenous movement in its raising awareness and facilitating developments at the regional level (Dahl 2012).

The ILO Convention No. 169 is the only legally binding instrument that deals with indigenous peoples on the international level. Among other things, the Convention safeguards the peoples' rights to their lands and participation in decision-making and development. However, altogether only 22 countries have ratified the Convention to date, and in a number of others—pro-human rights countries with indigenous populations—ratification is still either only under consideration or a non-issue altogether (International Labour Organization 2017). For example, of the Nordic countries with Saami population, forming a people whose traditional homeland covers Northwest Russia and the northern parts of Finland, Sweden and Norway, only Norway has ratified the Convention; it did so back in 1990. Another case is that of the Inuit. They are an indigenous people living in northern Canada, Alaska (USA), Russia and Greenland (Denmark), yet only Denmark has ratified the Convention, in 1996. As the critical literature on the challenges encountered at the national level in getting the Convention ratified has shown (e.g. Larsen 2016; Heinämäki et al. 2017), international political developments that would have any legally binding effect in indigenous issues are yet to come.

The lack of legally binding instruments notwithstanding, the recognition of indigenous peoples' political agency has been considered vital in both the international human rights framework and political processes. For example, ILO 169 highlights the importance of indigenous peoples' participation in decision-making, land issues and environmental, social and economic developments at large. The peoples themselves have also advocated for their inclusion in environmental management and sustainable development and the utilization of their knowledge in these areas (Heinämäki 2010). To this end and to promote their full and active participation in politics, the peoples have established their own international cross-border organizations, examples being the Saami Council, created in the 1950s, and the Inuit Circumpolar Council, founded in the 1970s. These organizations work to increase the visibility of the peoples internationally and to complement bodies with exclusively national mandates in order to promote the peoples' rights. The Saami Council, for example, provides a framework for the Saami in Russia, Finland, Sweden and Norway to come together as one people, whereas the Saami Parliaments (Sámediggi) in Finland, Sweden and Norway operate within their national political and legal frameworks. All in all, the permanent inclusion of the peoples in the structures of international institutions and the peoples' active role in claiming their rights have resulted in the peoples now unquestionably being seated at the 'tables' of global politics.

The political sites of indigenous inclusion that are of particular interest in this book are the UN Permanent Forum and the Arctic Council. *The UN Permanent Forum* was created to coordinate and integrate indigenous issues in the UN system. It is an advisory expert body, established in 2000, under the Economic and Social Council (ECOSOC), one of the UN's principal bodies along with the Security Council and the General Assembly. The Permanent Forum's position under the ECOSOC gives it a broad mandate in terms of the topics to be addressed. The Forum's tasks include formulating recommendations to the ECOSOC, UN agencies, states, indigenous and civil society organizations, private-sector actors and the media (Handbook for Participants 2007). Also noteworthy is the Forum's composition, a novel and much-celebrated feature. It consists of 16 expert members—eight state- and eight indigenous-nominated—all of whom have an equal position. Yet another key element is the open-door policy in the Forum's annual sessions whereby any indigenous organization that wishes to participate is welcome.

Since 2002, the Permanent Forum has held annual ten-day annual sessions that have become the largest international gathering of the world's indigenous peoples, with more than 1000 representatives attending (UN Division for Social Policy and Development 2017). As well as indigenous peoples' organizations and indigenous parliaments, the participants in the sessions represent member states, civil society organizations and academia (Handbook for Participants 2007). An important part of the annual gathering is the lobbying work done by indigenous peoples' organizations outside the formal meetings. In addition, various thematic side-events take place during the ten days. As an expert body, the Forum does not have a mandate to make decisions. Rather, it gathers and disseminates information, raises awareness and enhances coordination and integration of indigenous issues within the UN.

The Arctic Council can be considered a regional equivalent of the Permanent Forum. Established in 1996, the Council is an intergovernmental forum that brings together Arctic states and representatives of indigenous peoples to address concerns and challenges affecting the region. According to the Arctic Human Development Report (2004, pp. 17–18), the region encompasses Alaska, the northern areas of Canada, Greenland, the Faroe Islands, Iceland, the northern areas of Russia and the northernmost counties of Norway, Sweden and Finland. The area accounts for approximately 8% of the surface of the earth.

The tasks of the Arctic Council resonate with its origins in the Arctic Environmental Protection Strategy (AEPS), set out in 1991, which undertook to map, measure and, ultimately, protect the region and its environment. Environmental agendas have broadened, and the Council has extended the relevant issue areas in the Arctic to include the social, cultural and economic challenges that northern communities face. As it stands, the Council has been described as an Arctic voice and a decision-shaping body in regional and global politics (e.g. Axworthy et al. 2012). Moreover, it has been viewed as an exemplar of broadening traditional state-centric understandings of political participation by including indigenous peoples in its work.

The Council has eight member states (the Nordic countries, Russia, the USA and Canada) and six indigenous peoples' organizations, which have the status of Permanent Participant. The organizations are the Arctic Athabaskan Council, Aleut International Association, Gwich'in Council International, Inuit Circumpolar Council, Russian Association of Indigenous Peoples of the North and Saami Council. The work of the Arctic

Council is also followed by several non-Arctic states and a number of intergovernmental, interparliamentary and non-governmental organizations that have been granted the status of Observer. The right to participate in the work of the Council is limited to the representatives of the member states, the Permanent Participants and the Observers, and these actors have effective opportunities to influence the Council's policies. As a result, indigenous peoples have a strong and acknowledged position as stakeholders in Arctic issues. The Arctic states also benefit from maintaining and developing cooperation with indigenous groups (Tennberg 1998; Wilson and Øverland 2007).

The Council has a more informal structure than comparable international bodies and it does not have decision-making power as such. The chairmanship of the Council rotates among the member countries every two years. Decisions are made by consensus and issued in the form of non-binding declarations, which are drafted in ministerial meetings held every second year. Declarations set out the future action of the Council, but the larger regional and global impact of the Council derives from knowledge production, concretized in the data and analyses provided by six expert groups. Through the work of the Council, indigenous peoples have, in a historical way, gained a politically recognized status as experts on the phenomena that take place in their life worlds.

Both of these forums have been described as exemplary, even exceptional, in providing political space for indigenous peoples' representatives (Heinämäki 2010; Shadian 2009). The forums share three distinctive features: they are international; they address social, environmental and economic issues at large; and they are spaces within which indigenous peoples may exert influence and take part in shaping decisions. Where the Arctic Council deals with issues related to the Arctic and attracts the participation of Arctic indigenous peoples, the Permanent Forum is a global gathering place, drawing indigenous representatives from all over the world. The special role of indigenous peoples in global debates on sustainable development has been affirmed by their participation in the Forum. In addition to formal inclusion in the UN system, the Permanent Forum has offered indigenous peoples a place to develop cooperation and political strategies among themselves. In contrast to the creation of the Permanent Forum, in the case of the Arctic Council participation of indigenous peoples was secured by according them a particular position from the outset, not through a later move to correct past dismissal of them and their issues. In addition, the way in which the Council has made environmental protection and scientific aspirations distinctive elements of Arctic politics (Nilsson 2007; Shadian and Tennberg 2009) has enabled indigenous issues to become recognized as relevant to development in the Arctic and the world at large. Indigenous peoples' historical knowledge, current observations and daily experience of, for example, environmental and social changes taking place have become integral facets of not only Arctic politics but also global discussions on development, climate change and sustainability. Previously, input on their part was considered irrelevant or insignificant.

Despite their progressive attitude toward the inclusion of indigenous peoples in international politics, both the Permanent Forum and the Arctic Council, as well as their promise of change in politics and its treatment of indigenous peoples, have been criticized. As consultative and decision-shaping bodies, the forums' political impact has been questioned: their mandate is to produce recommendations that they do not have the tools to implement or monitor in practice. They have also been accused of being state-centric and bureaucratic (Lindroth 2006, 2011; Heininen and Numminen 2011). Nevertheless, these shortcomings have not diminished the role of either body as providing indigenous peoples with new opportunities for participation and exerting influence. The criticism raised by the peoples toward the limited leverage offered by these state-led political institutions, as well as calls for resurgence (Alfred and Corntassel 2004; Niezen 2009; Coulthard 2014), has not resulted in the peoples walking away from these opportunities, as limited as these may be.

Sketching Global Indigeneity

The transformation of international law and politics to become inclusive of indigenous peoples and their causes has triggered growing use of the term 'indigeneity'. The fairly recently gained recognition of indigenous peoples (lacking) rights and their historically oppressed position is in line with a universal perception of the peoples as a collective with a shared experience of dispossession and of being deprived basic human rights. The global perception of what indigenous peoples have been deprived of, how they identify themselves and differ from others and how they have been treated historically has given rise to the notion of 'indigeneity' as a common denominator that validates the peoples' claims and presence in politics and before the law.

The history and development of the concept of indigeneity has been a two-way street. On the one hand, the international legal framework introduced the term 'indigenous' to refer to a distinct group or community of people in order to define those in need of protection. One of the earliest appearances of the term was in the documents of the International Labour Organization (ILO) in the 1950s. Before that, it did not normally apply to describe people but flora and fauna native to a specific area. The human rights efforts of the ILO on behalf of the peoples in its Convention No. 107 Concerning the Protection and Integration of Indigenous and Other Tribal and Semi-Tribal Populations in Independent Counties, from 1957, marked a surge in the use of the term. In what was an era of assimilation, the views of the indigenous peoples themselves had been given no part in these legal and political considerations (Niezen 2009, p. 27). On the other hand, it did not take long for the indigenous peoples, struggling to make their causes heard in the international political and legal debate, to adopt the term and to utilize it for their own political purposes. If the political and legal mechanisms of that time were particularly keen on making a distinction between 'Settlers' and 'Natives' in societies, so were the peoples themselves, as the distinction served to highlight their lack of rights and protection. For the world's indigenous peoples claiming their rights, recognition of their cultural losses and redress for the wrongdoings of the past, 'indigenous' as a term denoting collectivity has provided the previously individual and domesticated struggles with global visibility and strength. After changing its take on indigenous issues from seeing them as domestic concerns to considering them causes for the international community, the United Nations has been the principal institutional home for the development of the concept of indigeneity, and it has provided a platform for indigenous peoples to meet and strategize (e.g. Merlan 2009; Dahl 2012). The recognition or acknowledgment of global indigeneity—as we see it today—has not, however, taken place without state affirmation.

The rubric 'indigeneity' binds together peoples through their considerable historical similarities of "settlement, colonization and marginalization" who on that basis have "moral claims on nation-states and on international society because of inhumane, unequal and exclusionary treatment" (Merlan 2009, p. 304). The term and its strategic use have been politically helpful for the peoples (Brysk 2000; Niezen 2003, 2009). The political currency of the term is linked to its relational nature, the ability to construct and create relations between the peoples as a joint force of various indigenous nations that align themselves to act as a unified counterforce to the states. Crystallizing the historical and current differences between indigenous people and the majority populations has been instrumental in order to 'close the gap' that exists between the peoples and the rest of the population in terms of rights, social and economic conditions and well-being. The term has succeeded in establishing this relationality as a difference that has political and legal significance (Merlan 2009, 2016).

Utilizing the construct of the 'global indigenous' as a platform to join forces and forge common claims has made it possible for indigenous peoples to build up their strength as an opposition to the power monopoly of the states. However, the construction of global indigeneity, or pan-indigeneity, by the political and legal systems as well indigenous peoples themselves has not come without strings attached. While it has provided political leverage, the assumption of a type of existence that is shared globally among the peoples and that could have 'indigenous' as a descriptive common denominator has also led to regional, historical and cultural nuances being overlooked. The focus on perceived commonalities in the peoples' cultural and historical backgrounds and the concomitant expectation of shared needs minimizes the heterogeneity of the peoples, their histories, experiences and needs. This simplification of the needs of those who have been marginalized, that is, the poor, refugees and the 'underdeveloped', among others, is characteristic of international politics, indigenous peoples and their situations being no exception. The less heartening side of the recognition of global indigeneity is that it ends up lumping together indigenous peoples from the rain forests of South America and the bushlands of Australia to the Canadian and Russian High Arctic. The term glosses over the diversity of the peoples' histories, current conditions and potential futures. Moreover, each of the peoples might exhibit great internal variety. All in all, little room is left for the whole spectrum of what indigeneity is, has been and could be. For all of its empowering and enabling facets, global indigeneity is also a rigid category that remains remote from the existing differences, diversity and messiness of lived realities.

Indeed, the initially well-meaning aim of the law to meet those it defines as Others and as being in need of protection has meant that the legal system has had to come up with a template schematizing those it seeks to protect. Thus, the category of 'indigenous' is a by-product of the benevolent attempts of the law to come to terms with the peoples' human rights. The acts of kindness done under the protective wing of the law and the rubric 'indigenous' are not, however, devoid of the more sinister workings of what is commonly perceived as justice. The power of international law, as seen in the conventions and declarations on indigeneity, lies in its having ultimate authority in setting the terms of recognition and in producing and defining the content of a category of identity. As critical legal scholars have noted, the capacity of law to govern is embedded in its exclusive authority to declare what is recognized before the law (Odysseos 2010; Sokhi-Bulley 2016). The paradoxes of cohesion-diversity and universality-particularity entailed in the legal definition of 'indigenous' reveal the problematic nature of the term. As Birrell (2016) has pointed out, there is a co-existing requirement of the peoples to be universally identifiable, yet culturally and geographically particular. That is, indigeneity as a category is needed both to demonstrate cohesiveness among the peoples and the peoples' distinctiveness from the rest of us (see also Niezen 2004). While 'indigenous' is a legally and politically compelling term, it is, at the same time, violent, disruptive and stagnant, especially in its constant reproduction of the distinction between those considered the 'norm' and those labeled the 'exception'.

We are aware of the power embedded in these concepts and acknowledge that 'indigeneity' and 'indigenous', as terms with a global purchase, trigger particular and to some extent problematic interpretations. However, in the practices, parlance and processes of international politics, such as those in the UN Permanent Forum and the Arctic Council, these are the concepts used when issues related to indigenous peoples and their political role are addressed. The two concepts hold their ground in our critical analysis of international politics and questions of indigeneity as our approach applies globally, beyond any individual site or the claims of any individual people. We also find ourselves bound to these concepts and their historical meanings, for we lack more nuanced, alternative terms free of the legal and political baggage that they have. Ultimately, we have opted to use 'indigenous' and 'indigeneity' rather interchangeably to describe the positions and positionings of the peoples in the contemporary political setting.

The Lingering Traces of Colonialism

The change or transformation that seems to have taken place in international politics is part of a series of events sparked by the world waking up to and trying to come to grips with its colonial heritage. It is rather recently that the white, Western and developed world changed its attitude toward its Others, those previously deprived of the blessings of 'civilized' humanity. At last, indigenous peoples, as well as women, people of color, people with mental and physical disabilities and those deemed to be of lower social class, have been considered worthy, at least by the minimum standards of human dignity. The institutional and legal changes on the international level have been beacons of hope for previously marginalized and dehumanized parts of the population. These changes have conveyed the image that the global community is willing to offer sanctuary to those still at the mercy of their colonial masters.

In this regard, the metaphor of home that Kofi Annan used in his speech to indigenous peoples in the first session of UN Permanent Forum in 2002 was a potent and salient one. Referring to a place of shelter, comfort and belonging was right on target for those who had been longing for such safety and affirmation from the global community in the midst of their colonial conditions. Colonialism was a conscious politics that aimed at diminishing, eroding and destroying ways of life and being that stood in the way of the colonial project or were irrelevant, useless, horrifying or repulsive to it. Where the colonial order found its subjects to have use and potential, especially in terms of financial profit, it allowed their existence—albeit as targets of assimilation, education and improvement. For indigenous peoples, colonial politics has meant numerous upheavals that have impacted their homes concretely. They have lost their homes and homeland due to forced relocation, confiscation and selling of their lands as well as policies that have allowed the slow decay of their dwellings by choosing to ignore their continuous presence there. They have lost ways of sustaining their homes: their opportunities to maintain traditional livelihoods have been denied, or severely compromised, as a result of losing lands, being moved around like chess pieces or having their immemorial fishing or hunting rights annulled. In equally severe developments, the peoples have lost future members due to forced child removals, Western education being imposed in boarding schools, lower life expectancy on reservations and policies of racial hygiene involving forced sterilizations. Their sense of home has been bruised by loss, disgrace and destruction of their traditional and sacred sites and the lands that have provided for them materially and spiritually. Similarly, the dignity and safety of their homes has been violated by acts of sexual, mental and physical abuse. In light of such considerations, an offering of an international 'home' by the leader of an established global institution was truly of great significance.

International politics finally, at least seemingly, confronting its acts of colonialism, the very events to which it has historically turned a blind eye, has marked an era of demonstrations of remorse and apologies. If colonialism meant openly unequal structures of domination, limited freedoms for some and a requirement that those under colonial rule adjust to the existing conditions in order to survive, the signs of progress and the inclusion of the peoples have been taken to mark the end of colonialism. The inclusion of indigenous peoples and the willingness to hear their histories and claims have signified such a period of trying to make amends. The peoples have been offered a home by granting them access to international institutions, providing platforms for states and indigenous peoples to come together on international ground and supporting the peoples' struggles for their rights through knowledge production and dissemination (Anaya 2004; Xanthaki 2007; Dahl 2012). As in the case of any home, the one offered to the peoples on the global level brings with it the promise of permanency; the peoples have a Permanent Forum in the UN and they are Permanent Participants in the Arctic Council.

With their heightened awareness of the international human rights system, states have taken it upon themselves to show that their stance on indigenous issues is in line with the global consciousness. Within the frame of sovereign nation-states, for example, special measures have been created allowing indigenous peoples to claim recognition as native inhabitants and, accordingly, rights to land (Knafla and Westra 2010). In this spirit the 2000s have seen states with large indigenous populations and considered to be pro-human rights, such as Australia, Canada and the USA, issue formal apologies to indigenous peoples. These apologies have named and specified, to varying degrees, the wrongdoings and responsibilities of the colonial states. Putting aside the question of what real and practical progress the apologies have produced, their core message has been to show remorse and a desire to make amends (Lightfoot 2015). Officially delivered state apologies to indigenous peoples have been considered as watersheds in the relations between the peoples and the states, events dividing these relations into the colonial ones 'before' and the more equal ones 'after', that is, those to come. Equally instrumental in redefining the relations between states and the peoples and facilitating processes of recompense have been the truth and reconciliation commissions in various countries, the latest additions being Finland and Norway and their relations with the Saami people (Barents Observer 2017a, b).

The UN Permanent Forum and the Arctic Council have been at the forefront in paving the way for indigenous peoples to have a more equal relationship with the states. The forums have offered the peoples seats at the tables of politics and, by doing so, suggested that there might be a concomitant redistribution of political power; this can be perceived as an act of remorse by the global community. The logic behind offering partnership to the peoples has been that states and global politics might make up for their colonial past through such organizational reforms and that this new alliance of states and the peoples would also translate into power actually being shared. In addition, the access of indigenous peoples to political and legal processes, as well as their current permanent position in international politics, in forums such as the UN Permanent Forum and the Arctic Council, can be interpreted as recognition of the special international status of the peoples (e.g. Morgan 2011).

This book takes issue with the idea(l)s that a change has occurred in global politics and that 'progress' necessarily means things improving for everyone. In particular, it questions the mindset that there has been an end to colonial patterns in contemporary global politics. Our main argument is that colonialism is still very much the order of the day, as it were, and we undertake to reveal how it operates by problematizing indigenous peoples' inclusion in international politics. In contrast to the literature that has viewed the inclusion of indigenous peoples in international politics as a milestone and an event that has drastically changed the course of politics, this book engages in a critical analysis of that institutional access, touted as seats of power being offered to the peoples. These forums, frequently referred to as exemplary, have brought to the fore, along with the promise of international politics redeeming its past, the expectation that the partnership between indigenous peoples and states will provide a future that is more just and equal—a future that is self-evidently worth pursuing and is freed from its colonial legacy.

We wish to note that by problematizing the extent to which this political partnership actually has changed the power setting, we do not mean to criticize the indigenous peoples' rightful involvement in global politics. Our critique targets the power setting of contemporary global politics, not the peoples' political representation and legal claims within that setting. Clearly, indigenous peoples, like other marginalized groups, should have an equally valid position in international politics among the rest of the human beings in the world. Problematizing the inclusion of indigenous peoples in international politics does not mean that the peoples should not be involved in that politics or that they should cease to utilize the current positions and possibilities that they have.

Our critical take on the peoples' inclusion in global politics stems from our respective and joint studies within the UN Permanent Forum and the Arctic Council. In the case of the UN Permanent Forum, on-site observations in the annual meetings, research interviews with indigenous peoples' and states' representatives and political statements in the sessions have offered perspectives on the process of inclusion of the peoples in the UN system (Lindroth 2015). In the context of the Arctic Council, the pioneering reports produced under its auspices, the meeting memoranda of one of its expert groups (Sustainable Development Working Group) and research interviews of the participants have painted a picture of the science-policy interaction and indigenous peoples' involvement in it (Sinevaara-Niskanen 2015). These materials have provided us with an in-depth view on the parlance and practices of the contemporary global politics that indigenous peoples have been invited to enter. Indeed, the depth and scope of the materials have illuminated the ways in which indigenous peoples and their issues have become included in yet, at the same time, excluded from the practices and agendas of politics.

Drawing on the perspectives provided by this material, we have concluded that the inclusive measures are mere sleight of hand aimed at cosmetically improving the face of global politics. The measures that symbolically and structurally seem to mark the end of exclusion are, in fact, premises through which the hierarchical, unequal and distortive techniques of power are allowed to live on. To describe this contemporary power, we consciously use the term 'colonialism' and thereby highlight how, despite global politics persuading us to think that colonialism is a thing of the past, it is very much alive in the present. As the impetus for the work stems from global politics and its efforts to atone and compensate for its colonial past, the discussions in this book are inspired by, but not tied to, the studies on the meanings and means of colonialism in different national settings today (e.g. Hale 2005; Coulthard 2014; Strakosch 2015; Veracini 2015; Postero 2017). 'Colonialism', like 'indigeneity', detached as it is from specific local contexts and having global purchase as a general concept, is based on commonalities in histories and experiences. For us, in the context of indigeneity and global politics, the common denominators of colonialism include hierarchical structures, processes of exclusion and biased political and legal systems. Our aim is to pinpoint some of the contemporary ways in which global politics, as an organic force with its own identifiable logic, continues to exercise power over indigeneity—power that fits comfortably under the umbrella term of colonialism. By turning the gaze toward the premises of the relations between indigenous peoples and states and the ways in which these relations are shaped, we wish to make visible the elephant that is still in the room, that is, colonial power. Therefore, this book deliberately flouts the prevailing global political parlance, in which it has become less popular to utter the word 'colonialism' and more appropriate to speak of partnership and 'moving on'.

The Biopolitical Present

In order to detail the ways in which the exercise of colonial power continues in global politics, we draw on critical discussions on neoliberalism and biopolitics. We argue that capturing how colonialism operates in relation to what has become an internationalized indigeneity requires an approach focusing on the techniques of governing indigeneity as a particular type of being and subjectivity. That is to say, the construction of global indigeneity—indigeneity that is based on collectivity and universality and that detaches itself from specific local conditions and characteristics—functions as a source on which the management of the peoples, their issues and agendas draws.

In the case of development at large, neoliberalism has come to rule as a rationale of organizing the world by economic parameters (Larner and Walters 2004; Walters 2012; Brown 2015). Neoliberal economics not only concerns issues of monetary profit and wealth per se but describes the ways in which management through competition, individual capacity-building, privatization and responsibilization has entered into all spheres of life. Issues ranging from social relations to health and personal safety are constructed, upheld and developed as sites of improvement and responsibility. If the world was once driven by an ambition to build political structures that would work for the common good, the introduction of neoliberal logic has meant a shift in focus from common to private and from providing security and well-being for all to promising it only to some.

The most noteworthy change that has followed the neoliberal turn is that the individual has become the bearer of responsibility for his or her own rights, living conditions and wealth. Achieving the security that was once at least promised, if not always actually provided, by society, is now wholly the responsibility of the neoliberal subject, who is 'active', 'entrepreneurial' and 'empowered' (Agrawal 2005; Larner 2005; Li 2007; Chandler and Reid 2016). Accordingly, the call for active indigenous agents has come to be a defining feature of global politics. Neoliberalism is reflected in the requirement that indigenous subjects draw on their own resources to participate, build their capacity and sustain and improve their lives (Odysseos 2010; Altamirano-Jiménez 2013).

The effort of the global community to make amends for the colonial past through inclusive measures has meshed neatly with the neoliberal rationality that nourishes active engagement and subjectivity, especially in the case of those that have been deprived of certain rights and privileges. For example, for the poor and dispossessed, the world has offered international development programs aimed at making them more capable of addressing and handling the situations that they face. For indigenous peoples, it has also created a special political category through which they may further their cause. The act of including indigenous peoples in global politics has suggested that the peoples might finally get their share of power. However, the inclusion of indigenous peoples, as we will detail later on, has been done in a manner that does not compromise the prevailing power positions of the states. While states seem to give some of their authority away for the benefit of the peoples, the benevolent processes of including the peoples are not devoid of fine-tuned neoliberal calculations of cost-effectiveness. Allowing indigenous peoples to enter as equals, which might have meant 'costs' to states in political leverage, is offset by the expectation of indigenous peoples committing themselves to consensuses as a political aim and to a growing political responsibility for their own historical, present and future conditions. Such expectations effectively control the peoples' political endeavors and agendas; that is, indigeneity becomes governed in a politically effective manner, one that follows the rationality of neoliberal economics.

Within the supposedly post-colonial but effectively neoliberal political space, the peoples have made their way as an active global collectivity. Within the given political setting, they have had to frame their political and legal claims in terms of past and continuous conditions of vulnerability, their environmental stewardship role and unique ability to cope. In particular, the peoples' allegedly close relationship to nature and their environmental observations have paved the way for them in global politics in an era when climate issues figure prominently. The political space accorded to the peoples on the basis of their special contributions to global politics has also meant that global indigeneity has become equated with certain features. Indigenous peoples are assumed to embody resilience, adaptability and care for the environment and community. It is these very features that are politically celebrated and cared for as the allegedly innate qualities of indigeneity. Indeed, the peoples' causes and stakeholdership have become acknowledged on the basis of these features, and it is through them that the peoples consciously seek to advance their political agendas.

If, as we argue, neoliberalism can help to explain the logic behind the simultaneous inclusion and exclusion of indigenous peoples in international politics and the call for their active participation, a biopolitical approach can unveil the ways in which the neoliberal emphasis on active agency secures a grip on indigenous subjectivity on a fundamental level. To our understanding, the very core on which the contemporary violent care for indigeneity draws consists of the features that international politics expects of indigeneity and that appears enabling. A shift has taken place from the past colonial corporeal brutalities to the contemporary biopolitical call for indigenous life and existence, which are politically pre-defined. This pre-definition means the selective acknowledgment, praise and valuing of indigeneity as resilient, adaptive and bound to the community. These criteria need to be met in order for indigeneity to claim entry into international politics. The nurturing and celebration of only certain types of indigenous living and being—while casting aside or ignoring others—is part and parcel of neoliberal power and its 'vital politics' (Lemke 2008; Lindroth and Sinevaara-Niskanen 2016).

The shift to include indigenous peoples and the quest for active agents have intensified the focus on indigeneity as a particular type of subjectivity that is either considered worthy or relegated to the category of 'irrelevant' and 'not fit for the purpose'. In the spheres of international politics, the resilient indigenous, for example, have become extremely relevant as the world wishes the peoples to show an example of how to adapt to and cope with the current and forthcoming changes. The desire for the eternally adaptive indigenous subject that accommodates itself to its given conditions as well as the political celebration of such alleged capacities is a singular way in which indigenous being is governed. The violence entailed in this contemporary biopolitical order is that it penetrates to the very heart of subjectivity, that is, of what indigeneity is required to be and how it is up to that subjectivity to correct and improve itself in order to cope with its conditions. The biopolitical move masks what has been a subtle shift of political attention from the circumstances of dispossession to the subject and its internal resources. The concern for the pre-defined and select indigeneity only—with a subject that fits the purposes of neoliberal rule—is tantamount to global politics being concerned and caring for a fantasized indigeneity. Removed from lived realities of indigenous peoples, the political fantasy of indigeneity is an artificial construction with which the peoples are forced to comply if they want to represent themselves, advance claims and argue for their rightful existence. Thus, in effect, the care of global politics for indigeneity is a colonial use of power targeting the indigenous subject.

We argue that the care of global politics for indigeneity is the contemporary wave of colonialism, a sequel to the past events. The apparent change for the better in political parlance, institutional reforms and the overall appearance of politics masks what was once a blatant use of power. The colonial setting seems to have been replaced with partnership and cooperation. These neoliberal techniques are not, however, any less flush with power hierarchies or efforts to control the peoples. On the contrary, the neoliberal apparatuses of empowerment and responsibilization have made the grip of global politics on indigeneity a powerful one. Through the biopolitical care for indigeneity, indigenous subjectivity has become the site of intervention and the surface on which contemporary colonialism etches its demands. In effect, global politics has retained its colonial mindset.

In order to elaborate our argument, we dissect the question of international politics and indigeneity by peeling off, layer by layer, the means and rationales of inclusion. Of the following chapters, Chap. 2 focuses on the institutional inclusion of indigenous peoples in the UN Permanent Forum and the Arctic Council. It examines the ways in which these forums have enabled, in a pioneering way, the participation of the peoples and how the involvement of indigenous peoples takes place in practice. Through its critique of neoliberal engagement, the chapter assesses the extent to which these measures of inclusion have actually made a difference and furthered the peoples' political position.

Chapters 3 and 4 discuss the principal ways in which indigeneity is perceived in contemporary global politics. Chapter 3 focuses on the notions of environmental boundedness, vulnerability and adaptation, which have come to circumscribe indigeneity. The chapter shows how these notions construct requirements of indigenous exceptionality that the peoples are to embrace in order to enter political arenas and debates. Taking this discussion further, Chap. 4 discusses the ways in which resilience—as a descriptive neoliberal term subsuming the peoples' (alleged) vulnerability, role as caretakers and adaptability—has taken over in international politics and its dealings with indigeneity. The chapter analyzes the requirement of resilient indigeneity as a neoliberal trope that has redirected the interventions, attention and measures of global politics from conditions to subjects. Instead of politics being concerned with amending the conditions that demand resilience on the part of indigenous subjects—conditions that the politics itself has caused—the politics of resilience is interested in enhancing the subjects that are struggling under those conditions. The chapter shows how this shift in focus is a move that dilutes the political potential of indigeneity to challenge the existing power set-up.

Continuing the discussion on the indigenous subject, Chap. 5 examines the ways in which indigenous being is governed biopolitically. It teases out three modes of biopolitical love toward indigeneity and reveals how this care is, in effect, violent in nature. It elaborates an analytical approach to determining the techniques by which the empathetic and loving care of indigeneity operates to detain that subjectivity in a position where it is eternally in the making. In particular, the chapter elaborates how biopolitical control over indigenous subjectivity, a contemporary colonialism, proceeds in new guises.

The concluding chapter, Chap. 6, summarizes our critique of the alleged progress made in indigenous issues in international politics. It shows, by exploding the myth of progress, how the control over indigeneity is, if possible, tighter than ever. It discusses how the benevolent attempts of contemporary global politics to include indigeneity are nothing more than quasi-responses that facilitate the ruling system's abdication of its responsibility. As the chapter asserts, by offering signals of hope and progress, international politics exhorts indigeneity, yet again, to wait and to be patient.

References

Agrawal, Arun. 2005. *Environmentality. Technologies of Government and the Making of Subjects.* Durham: Duke University Press.

Alfred, Taaiake, and Jeff Corntassel. 2004. *A Decade of Rhetoric for Indigenous Peoples?* http://www.corntassel.net/print_rhetoric.htm. Accessed 9 May 2017.

Altamirano-Jiménez, Isabel. 2013. Indigenous Encounters with Neoliberalism. In *Place, Women and the Environmental in Canada and Mexico.* Vancouver: UBC Press.

Anaya, James. 2004. *Indigenous Peoples in International Law.* 2nd ed. Oxford: Oxford University Press.

Arctic Human Development Report. 2004. Akyreyri: Stefansson Arctic Institute.

Axworthy, Timothy S., Timo Koivurova, and Waliul Hasanat, eds. 2012. *The Arctic Council: Its Place in the Future of Arctic Governance.* Toronto: Walter & Duncan Gordon Foundation.

Barents Observer. 2017a. *Truth and Reconciliation Commission May Be Launched in Finland Already After Summer.* https://thebarentsobserver.com/en/life-and-public/2017/05/truth-and-reconciliation-commission-may-be-launched-finland-already-after. Accessed 12 May 2017.

———. 2017b. *Political Support for Norwegian Truth and Reconciliation Commission*. https://thebarentsobserver.com/en/life-and-public/2017/06/political-support-norwegian-truth-and-reconciliation-commission#.WTltZBUmBe4.twitter. Accessed 10 June 2017.

Barnett, Michael, and Martha Finnemore. 2005. The Power of Liberal International Organizations. In *Power in Global Governance*, ed. Michael Barnett and Raymont Duvall, 161–184. Cambridge: Cambridge University Press.

Birrell, Kathleen. 2016. *Indigeneity: Before and Beyond the Law*. Abingdon: Routledge.

Brown, Wendy. 2015. *Undoing the Demos: Neoliberalism's Stealth Revolution*. New York: Zone Books.

Brysk, Alison. 2000. *From Tribal Village to Global Village: Indian Rights and International Relations in Latin America*. Stanford: Stanford University Press.

Chandler, David, and Julian Reid. 2016. *The Neoliberal Subject. Resilience, Adaptation and Vulnerability*. London: Rowman & Littlefield.

Corntassel, Jeff. 2008. Toward Sustainable Self-Determination: Rethinking the Contemporary Indigenous-Rights Discourse. *Alternatives* 33: 105–132.

Coulthard, Glen Sean. 2014. *Red Skin, White Masks. Rejecting the Colonial Politics of Recognition*. Minneapolis: University of Minnesota Press.

Dahl, Jens. 2012. *Indigenous Space and Marginalized Peoples in the United Nations*. New York: Palgrave Macmillan.

Hale, Charles R. 2005. Neoliberal Multiculturalism: The Remaking of Cultural Rights and Racial Dominance in Central America. *PoLAR: Political and Legal Anthropology Review* 28 (1): 10–28.

Handbook for Participants. 2007. United Nations Permanent Forum on Indigenous Issues. http://www.un.org/esa/socdev/unpfii/documents/guide_participants_en.pdf. Accessed 19 June 2017.

Heinämäki, Leena. 2010. *The Right to Be a Part of Nature: Indigenous Peoples and the Environment*. Rovaniemi: Lapland University Press. http://lauda.ulapland.fi/bitstream/handle/10024/61694/Hein%c3%a4m%c3%a4kiDORIA.pdf?sequence=3&isAllowed=y. Accessed 21 June 2017.

Heinämäki, Leena, Christina Allard, Stefan Kirchner, Alexandra Xanthaki, Sanna Valkonen, Ulf Mörkenstam, Nigel Bankes, Jacinta Ruru, Jéremie Gilbert, Per Selle, Audra Simpson, and Laura Olsén. 2017. *Actualizing Sámi Rights: International Comparative Research*. Publications of the Government's analysis, assessment and research activities 4/2017. Prime Minister's Office. http://tietokayttoon.fi/documents/10616/3866814/4_Saamelaisten+oikeuksien+toteutuminen+kansainv%C3%A4linen+oikeusvertaileva+tutkimus/e765f819-d90c-4318-9ff0-cf4375e00688?version=1.0. Accessed 22 June 2017.

Heininen, Lassi, and Lotta Numminen. 2011. Suomi arktisena maana ja Euroopan unioinin jäsenvaltiona: Miten Arktista neuvostoa vahvistetaan. In *Jäitä poltellessa*.

Suomi ja arktisen alueen tulevaisuus, ed. Lassi Heininen and Teemu Palosaari, 131–142. Tampere: TAPRI Studies in Peace and Conflict Research.

Indigenous Peoples' Center for Documentation, Research and Information. 2017. The Six Nations of the Iroquois at the League of Nations: 1923–1933. http://cendoc.docip.org/cgi-bin/library.cgi?e=p-00100-00---off-0--00----0-10-0---0---0direct-10----4-------0-1l--10-en-50---20-home---0--1-00-10--4----0-0-01-10-0utfZz-8-00&a=p&p=about&c=deskaheh. Accessed 26 Apr 2017.

International Labour Organization. 2017. Ratifications of C169 – Indigenous and Tribal Peoples Convention, 1989 (No. 169). http://www.ilo.org/dyn/normlex/en/f?p=NORMLEXPUB:11300:0::NO::P11300_INSTRUMENT_ID:312314. Accessed 3 July 2017.

Knafla, Louis A., and Haijo Westra. 2010. *Aboriginal Title and Indigenous Peoples: Canada, Australia, and New Zealand*. Vancouver: UBC Press.

Larner, Wendy. 2005. Neoliberalism in (Regional) Theory and Practice: the Stronger Communities Action Fund in New Zealand. *Geographical Research* 43 (1): 9–18.

Larner, Wendy, and William Walters, eds. 2004. *Global Governmentality: Governing International Spaces*. London: Routledge.

Larsen, Peter Bille. 2016. The 'New Jungle Law': Development, Indigenous Rights and ILO Convention 169 in Latin America. *International Development Policy* 7 (1). https://poldev.revues.org/2220. Accessed 4 July 2017.

Lemke, Thomas with Stephanie Baele. 2008. An Interview with Thomas Lemke: Foucault Today. On the Theoretical Relevance of Foucauldian Concepts of 'Governmentality' and 'Biopolitics'. *Emulations* 2(4). http://www.revue-emulations.net/interviews/interviews2/thomaslemke-foucaulttoday. Accessed 30 June 2017.

Li, Tania Murray. 2007. *The Will to Improve. Governmentality, Development, and the Practice of Politics*. Durham: Duke University Press.

Lightfoot, Sheryl. 2015. Settler-State Apologies to Indigenous Peoples: A Normative Framework and Comparative Assessment. *Native American and Indigenous Studies* 2 (1): 15–39.

Lindroth, Marjo. 2006. Indigenous-State Relations in the UN: Establishing the Indigenous Forum. *Polar Record* 42 (3): 239–248.

———. 2011. Paradoxes of Power: Indigenous Peoples in the Permanent Forum. *Cooperation and Conflict* 46 (4): 542–561.

———. 2015. *Governing Indigeneity Globally: Indigenous Peoples in the United Nations*. Rovaniemi: Lapland University Press.

Lindroth, Marjo, and Heidi Sinevaara-Niskanen. 2016. The Biopolitics of Resilient Indigeneity and the Radical Gamble of Resistance. *Resilience: International Policies, Practices and Discourses* 4 (2): 130–145.

Merlan, Francesca. 2009. Indigeneity. Global and Local. *Current Anthropology* 50 (3): 303–333.

———. 2016. Indigeneity in Australia: National and International Dimensions. Manuscript under review.

Morgan, Rhiannon. 2011. *Transforming Law and Institution: Indigenous Peoples, the United Nations and Human Rights*. Farnham: Ashgate.

Niezen, Ronald. 2003. *The Origins of Indigenism. Human Rights and the Politics of Identity*. Berkeley: University of California Press.

———. 2004. *A World Beyond Difference. Cultural Identity in the Age of Globalization*. Malden: Blackwell Publishing.

———. 2009. *The Rediscovered Self. Indigenous Identity and Cultural Justice*. Montreal: McGill-Queen's University Press.

Nilsson, Annika E. 2007. *A Changing Arctic Climate. Science and Policy in the Arctic Climate Impact Assessment*. Linköping Studies in Arts and Science No. 386. Linköping: Linköping University, Department of Water and Environmental Studies.

Odysseos, Louiza. 2010. Human Rights, Liberal Ontogenesis and Freedom: Producing a Subject for Neoliberalism? *Millennium: Journal of International Studies* 38 (3): 747–772.

Postero, Nancy. 2017. *The Indigenous State: Race, Politics, and Performance in Plurinational Bolivia*. Oakland: University of California Press.

Shadian, Jessica M. 2009. Revisiting Politics and Science in the Poles: IPY and the Governance of Science in Post-Westphalia. In *Legacies and Change in Polar Science. Historical, Legal and Political Reflections on the International Polar Year*, ed. Jessica M. Shadian and Monica Tennberg, 35–62. Surrey: Ashgate.

Shadian, Jessica M., and Monica Tennberg, eds. 2009. *Legacies and Change in Polar Science. Historical, Legal and Political Reflections on the International Polar Year*. Surrey: Ashgate.

Sinevaara-Niskanen, Heidi. 2015. *Setting the Stage for Arctic Development: Politics of Knowledge and the Power of Presence*. Rovaniemi: Lapland University Press.

Sokhi-Bulley, Bal. 2016. *Governing (Through) Rights*. Oxford: Hart Publishing.

Strakosch, Elizabeth. 2015. *Neoliberal Indigenous Policy: Settler Colonialism and the 'Post-Welfare' State*. London: Palgrave Macmillan.

Tennberg, Monica. 1998. *The Arctic Council. A Study in Governmentality*. Rovaniemi: University of Lapland.

UN Division for Social Policy and Development. 2017. *News: Permanent Forum Concludes with Call to Action and Report*. https://www.un.org/development/desa/indigenouspeoples/news/2017/05/un-permanent-forum-on-indigenous-issues-concludes-with-call-to-action/. Accessed 8 May 2017.

UN Secretary General. 2002. *Press Release: 'You Have a Home at the United Nations,' Says Secretary-General, as Indigenous Forum Concludes First Session*. http://www.un.org/press/en/2002/sgsm8249.doc.htm. Accessed 3 July 2017.

Veracini, Lorenzo. 2015. *The Settler Colonial Present*. Basingstoke: Palgrave Macmillan.

Walters, William. 2012. *Governmentality. Critical Encounters*. London: Routledge.

Wilson, Elana, and Indra Øverland. 2007. Indigenous Issues. In *International Cooperation and Arctic Governance. Regime Effectiveness and Northern Region Building*, ed. Olav Schram Stokke and Geir Hønneland, 27–49. New York: Routledge.

Xanthaki, Alexandra. 2007. *Indigenous Rights and United Nations Standards: Self-Determination, Culture and Land*. Cambridge: Cambridge University Press.

CHAPTER 2

Excluded in the Past, Celebrated in the Present

Making International Politics 'Better'

The inclusion of indigenous peoples and attention to their issues in political forums such as the UN Permanent Forum on Indigenous Issues and the Arctic Council can be traced to the long history of indigenous peoples demanding to be heard and included in international politics. Extensive processes of decolonization, the emergence of pro-human rights attitudes and the civil rights movements of the 1960s and 1970s buoyed the indigenous struggles for rights and recognition and the establishment of networks among the peoples (Niezen 2003; García-Alix 2003). The UN has been the platform of choice for forging a 'better' politics that is more inclusive, just, reciprocal and humane to all those parts of populations that have been ill-treated, excluded and have suffered injustices. By the same token, the organization has been instrumental in creating and nourishing the global indigenous movement.

A significant change has taken place in international society's orientation toward indigenous peoples since the first initiatives a century ago that saw indigenous peoples appeal to and be rejected by that political community. The Working Group on Indigenous Populations (WGIP), established in 1982, was the first official channel for indigenous peoples to enter the UN and international politics. The pressure brought to bear by the strong global indigenous movement, along with states' increasing inclination to make amends for their colonial past, led to a major study on the discrimination

M. Lindroth, H. Sinevaara-Niskanen, *Global Politics and Its Violent Care for Indigeneity*,
https://doi.org/10.1007/978-3-319-60982-9_2

against indigenous peoples. The study, known as the Cobo Report (1983), was conducted over many years, starting in the 1970s and publishing its final report in 1983. The Cobo Report revealed the need for special measures to eliminate discrimination both on a country level and in the UN system. It became evident that the rights developed for minority groups—facilitated by the UN—could not adequately meet the needs of indigenous peoples, who had come to be understood as more than 'just' minorities. This special situation, as the report noted, had to be acknowledged and the peoples granted a position enabling them to have a say on issues affecting them. The Working Group was an answer to the call for greater involvement and an improved opportunity to be heard.

The WGIP put forward a two-pronged proposal for the special measures needed to improve the situation of indigenous peoples, within the UN system itself as well as globally. First, in the area of political participation, the Working Group introduced the principle of open participation for any indigenous NGO, embraced 20 years later by the UN Permanent Forum on Indigenous Issues. Significantly, the establishment of the WGIP also marked a change in the UN itself, as it entailed the creation of an entirely new body on its organizational chart. To be sure, this change would not have taken place without indigenous peoples' vocal activism demanding more opportunities for participation.

Second, in terms of the substance of its work, the Working Group was tasked with drafting the Declaration on the Rights of Indigenous Peoples (UNDRIP), an instrument designed to affirm and protect the collective and individual rights of indigenous peoples. The draft was debated in the UN system for two decades before finally being adopted by the General Assembly in 2007. The UNDRIP has been considered one of the most significant UN advances where indigenous peoples are concerned. By bringing universal human rights into the special context of indigenous peoples, it codifies the rights of the peoples to the extent to which the international community of states has recognized them. It is seen as articulating a minimum standard of achievement to be pursued (Wiessner 2009, p. 3).

Other reforms within the UN system can be cited that are often seen as signifying recognition of the special international status of indigenous peoples alongside the institutional changes and legal advances noted above (e.g. Morgan 2011). In one reform, in 2001, the Commission on Human Rights established the position of Special Rapporteur on the Rights of Indigenous Peoples (SRIP). The Special Rapporteur promotes good practices and implements international standards for the rights of indigenous peoples, reports on the human rights situation of the peoples, addresses violations of these rights and conducts thematic studies. To date, the position has been held by three experts on the social, cultural, legal, political and economic situations of indigenous peoples (Office of the United Nations High Commissioner for Human Rights 2017a). In 2007, as part of a more extensive reform and the establishment of the Human Rights Council, the WGIP was replaced by the Expert Mechanism on the Rights of Indigenous Peoples. This body has five members who are experts on indigenous rights, and it is mandated to provide the Human Rights Council with thematic advice. The Expert Mechanism holds sessions in which interested parties, such as indigenous peoples and states, may participate (Office of the United Nations High Commissioner for Human Rights 2017b).

The initial access gained through the Working Group on Indigenous Populations led to indigenous peoples acquiring the status of legitimate participants in the UN processes and more broadly. Among other benefits, the institutional recognition by the UN has enabled indigenous peoples to create their own forms of cooperation, such as the Global Indigenous Caucus, which is important for joint strategizing and negotiation between indigenous groups. Some have even stated that 'an indigenous space' has been created in the UN (Dahl 2012).

The establishment of the Permanent Forum was a natural continuation of developments taking place in the UN at the time. The aim was to build more coordinated efforts to address, work on and improve the situation of indigenous peoples. The first mention of a permanent indigenous forum was heard back in the early days of indigenous peoples' involvement in the UN. Furthermore, it had become clear over time that the UN needed to better coordinate its work on issues pertaining to indigenous peoples (Søvndahl Petersen 1999, p. 9). Upon its establishment, the Permanent Forum was hailed as an unprecedented reform in the UN system, one that would put indigenous issues on the organization's agenda permanently and make them an integral part of its work. Indeed, the Forum was an answer to the call for a permanent body—one primarily demanded by indigenous peoples themselves—that would address indigenous issues in what was a global arena and, importantly, offer indigenous peoples access and inclusion. In this respect, the establishment of the Permanent Forum has accomplished its initial aim.

In an important feature as regards inclusion, any indigenous NGO is welcome to participate in the sessions of the Permanent Forum, which convene once a year over a period of ten working days. This policy is vitally important for the legitimacy of the Forum. Those participating include representatives of not only indigenous peoples and indigenous parliaments but also of state and UN agencies, civil society organizations and academia. Participants in the annual sessions can deliver statements in the plenary session on the mandated issue areas. More important than the formal sessions are the joint strategizing among indigenous groups, negotiations with states, the informal lobbying, discussions and politics that go on outside the formal sessions and the opportunity to bring shame upon states when necessary (Lindroth 2011). Indeed, the Forum has taken its place as a significant gathering of the world's indigenous peoples, and its annual sessions boast an attendance of some 1200 people (Handbook for Participants 2007; UN Division for Social Policy and Development 2017).

The extensive and varied attendance increases the political—and moral—weight of the Forum. The participation of representatives of indigenous peoples and of the many civil society organizations working with and promoting the peoples' rights contributes to answering the calls for a more inclusive and just politics in the UN. To judge from the large number of participants, it seems that the Forum has been able to build a more inclusive environment and that this inclusion was, indeed, lacking. The Forum has further strengthened the importance of the UN as the foremost political arena for the global indigenous peoples' movement.

The significant novelty in how the work of the Permanent Forum is organized is that all the experts—indigenous-nominated and state-appointed alike—work on an equal footing. This is often regarded as a milestone in the politics between indigenous peoples and states. Of the 16 experts in the Forum who draft recommendations to the Economic and Social Council (ECOSOC), states and other UN organizations, half are nominated by indigenous peoples and half by states. States first submit a list of nominees, from which the ECOSOC selects delegates based on five regional groupings of states. Indigenous organizations also submit nominees, and the final delegates are chosen by the president of the ECOSOC based on seven socio-cultural regions and consultations with indigenous organizations. The experts are expected to cooperate and act independently on behalf of the Forum, not to represent the interests of any particular state or indigenous group. The shared thematic leadership of the experts is one of the key mechanisms in making the body appear just. Of particular importance for indigenous peoples is that the body not only looks out for the interests of states but also takes indigenous representatives structurally on board as equal partners.

Indeed, even though the Forum is an expert body in that it does not have any decision-making power, it plays a significant role in raising awareness, shaping opinion, disseminating information and foregrounding issues that are deemed important internationally. The mandate of the Permanent Forum includes all the areas covered by the ECOSOC: economic and social development, culture, environment, education, health and human rights. The broad array of issues that the work of the Forum spans adds to its political weight. Because of its broad mandate and global visibility, the Forum and the knowledge and networks it has engendered have provided the peoples with a better position in negotiations that take place locally.

Similarly, the Arctic Council has been described as a political body for decision-shaping, not decision-making. Born of efforts to promote cooperation, coordination and interaction in the Arctic, the Council has been hailed as "institutional experimentation" and an "innovative approach" in governing development in the region (Arctic Human Development Report 2004, p. 237). The establishment of the Council in 1996 can be considered one trickle-down effect of global politics acknowledging the political role of indigenous peoples, a trend reflected in the UN in particular. Several years before the establishment of the Council, the Arctic Environmental Protection Strategy (AEPS) noted the presence and contribution of indigenous peoples in the Arctic area. However, it was the establishment of the Council, its work underpinned by the AEPS, that ultimately made the role of the peoples in the region institutionally visible. Arctic indigenous peoples were included in the structures of the Council from the outset. It currently has six indigenous peoples' organizations, which have the status of Permanent Participant, that geographically cover the entire Arctic. To become a Permanent Participant, an indigenous organization must represent either one indigenous peoples living in more than one Arctic state or several indigenous peoples living in a single state. For example, the Inuit Circumpolar Council (ICC) represents the Inuit living in Greenland, Alaska, Canada and Russia, whereas the Russian Association of Indigenous Peoples of the North is the voice for a variety of indigenous groups in northern Russia.

The indigenous participants have equal footing with the eight member states—the Nordic countries, Russia, USA and Canada—in the work of the Arctic Council. The Permanent Participants have full rights to participate and to obtain information in the Council's proceedings and negotiations. Indigenous representatives take part in the meetings together with member states, organizations and non-Arctic states that have been granted the status of Observer as well as any specialists invited to contribute to the Council's work. Even before the establishment of the Council and during the negotiations on the Arctic Environmental Protection Strategy, the Indigenous Peoples' Secretariat (IPS) was created to facilitate indigenous peoples' participation. The Secretariat supports the work of the peoples by, for example, providing them with background information, recent research findings and assisting them in policy processes. The IPS also functions as a platform for cooperation between indigenous organizations. This institutional support has been designed to ensure that indigenous peoples have genuine possibilities to take part in the work of the Council.

The international organization of the Council is informal. Decisions are drafted in ministerial meetings held every second year and published in the form of declarations, which set out the future actions of the Council. Declarations are not binding, and there are few regulations on how the Council's decisions should be implemented. The day-to-day operations of the Council are managed by Senior Arctic Officials, a body comprising the polar or Arctic ambassadors of the Council's member countries (Axworthy et al. 2012; Hønneland and Stokke 2007). As environmental protection and scientific aspirations have been, and continue to be, distinctive focuses of the Council, much of its work takes place in specialized working groups. There are six such groups, each with a specific profile and historical background, originating in either the AEPS or more recent regional concerns: the Arctic Monitoring and Assessment Program, Conservation of Arctic Flora and Fauna, Emergency Prevention, Preparedness and Response, Protection of the Arctic Marine Environment, the Sustainable Development Working Group and Arctic Contaminants Action Program. While indigenous peoples' organizations are involved on an equitable basis in the work of all of the groups, the highly specialized nature of the work done in some of them has posed challenges to some of the indigenous representatives in observing and contributing to the discussions.

In practice, the working groups of the Council operate by carrying out projects. For example, the projects of the Sustainable Development Working Group (SDWG), established in 1998 with the aim of addressing the social dimensions of Arctic concerns, are endorsed and approved by the Senior Arctic Officials of the member countries. As the SDWG is the forum which carries out the Council's work on social, economic and cultural development of the region, its agenda and the scope of its projects are broad, encompassing questions of indigenous languages, health and well-being, cultural rights and education. Many indigenous representatives have considered it essential to participate in the work of the SDWG and its projects due to the comprehensive range of issues it addresses, issues of critical social and cultural importance. The SDWG has produced some of the leading documents providing information on human development in the Arctic region, such as the Arctic Human Development Reports published in 2004 and 2015.

All in all, the Council has carved itself a particular "cognitive niche" (Stokke 2007, p. 18) in global politics by providing information that has been lacking and by taking the lead in furthering issues deemed important to the region. The inclusion of indigenous peoples in the Council, and particularly the opportunities to produce knowledge this has brought, has provided the peoples with possibilities to impact politics on a circumpolar scale.

In global perspective, the Arctic Council and the Permanent Forum represent singular attempts to respond to calls for making politics 'better' and altering the points of departure that have historically been distorted, biased and exclusive. Both of the forums have been exemplary in recognizing indigenous peoples' rightful presence in political arenas and discussions that are global in scale. The developments within the UN system to improve the situation of the peoples and the visibility of their causes have been instrumental in increasing global awareness. Conversely, the global awareness achieved has impacted regional politics and processes. Crucial to all the advances has been indigenous peoples' own activism. What is more, their perseverance in claiming equal footing in politics concerning them has set the stage for the process of redemption for the global political community and the states that have previously turned their backs on the peoples. Institutional inclusion of the peoples and consideration of their issues have been among the key ways of starting to 'fix' injustices and to make politics appear a changed game.

The Desire to Make Amends: But Some Things Cannot Be 'Fixed'

The inclusion of indigenous peoples and their agendas has been one of the ways in which international politics has sought to make amends with the peoples. Attempts to correct the wrongdoings of the past resonate with the emerging change in the mindset of the international community and the moral and political pressure brought to bear by indigenous peoples. The Permanent Forum and the Arctic Council have been celebrated for their work as examples of making a new type of international politics that builds on recognition, equality and partnership between indigenous peoples, states and the international community at large. The underpinning idea is that a shift in politics has taken place in attitudes and the distribution of power toward better political systems that genuinely take previously excluded peoples under their wing.

Inclusion has been a response by the international community to criticism that indigenous peoples have been excluded. What the peoples once lacked they now seem to have: access and institutional inclusion, venues for networking, possibilities to exert influence and moral and political leverage in international political arenas. To date, the inclusion of indigenous peoples in international politics, both in the UN Permanent Forum and the Arctic Council, has been considered a significant sign of progress. The type of inclusion that these forums have enabled for indigenous peoples continues to be admired, despite the occasional criticism, for example, that the inclusion rests on state-based and state-run administrative machinery. Yet, alarmingly little debate can be cited on the extent to which, and how, the inclusion of the peoples in political structures built by the powers who colonized them can resolve the peoples' colonial dispossession (on notable exceptions, see; Alfred 2005; Corntassel 2008; Lindroth and Sinevaara-Niskanen 2013). Such developments toward more inclusive politics are not without merit, but on what level can institutional inclusion redress injustices and dispossession?

The initial eye-opener and impetus prompting us to view inclusion more critically was that despite all the positive developments in the rights and political participation of indigenous peoples, the peoples still find themselves in marginal positions—positions that this very inclusion was meant to eliminate. The peoples' rights continue to be violated or are completely lacking, an example of the latter being the rights to their lands, now the crux of indigenous struggles around the globe. Even the pioneers of inclusion, the Permanent Forum and the Arctic Council, despite accommodating critical discussion on the situation of indigenous peoples, have not been able to remedy such situations. The concerns raised by indigenous peoples during the early stages of these arenas are still center stage in their proceedings as the issues are yet to be resolved.

For example, the question of how indigenous peoples could fully deploy their existing participatory rights continues to be discussed in the respective organizations. In the UN today, 2017, one still sees calls for indigenous participants to be consulted on the processes and procedures by which they are included in the work of the body. On the basis of these calls, it is clear that structural inclusion has not removed the manifold barriers to the peoples having their voices heard. Yet another process assessing the peoples' position was launched on 3 October 2016 at the UN, with the hope expressed that the peoples would actively take part (UN Letter of Invitation for Indigenous Peoples 2016). Tellingly, even in the UN, indigenous peoples' participation—despite its structurally permanent basis—is still in need of support and evaluation. Similarly, Finland's chairmanship program for the Arctic Council for 2017–2019 states that "Finland *supports* the strong participation of indigenous peoples in the work of the Arctic Council and the *integration* of traditional and local knowledge into the programs and projects of the Council" (Finland's Chairmanship Program 2017–2019, p. 14, emphasis added). As the wording suggests, even though the peoples have been legitimate participants in the Council from the beginning, their political position is still in need of enhancing. Their full-fledged participation and the integration of their agendas are yet to be achieved and, thus, the peoples, their causes and agency are in need of support. The other topics discussed in these forums, issues that are never exhausted, include indigenous peoples' lack of funding and support for their languages and cultures, the comparatively lower living conditions of indigenous peoples—even in many First World countries—and control over the use of natural resources in indigenous territories.

Indeed, it is controversial that international politics offers inclusion as the solution that would overcome the marginalization and subjugation that the international community's colonial past has caused. Indigenous peoples have been described as dispossessed, wounded and victimized. Theirs is a position marked by a fundamental lack of rights, resources and recognition. As Alfred notes, colonization has affected and continues to affect indigenous peoples through the imposition of "a perpetual colonized victim way of life and view of the world" (Alfred 2005, p. 25). It is from this position of weakness that indigenous peoples enter the negotiations in international politics. Similarly, as Birrell (2010) has pointed out, legal recognition is built on a presumption that indigenous peoples are in "scars" and "lacerated." This scarring is a prerequisite for them to become identified and, thus, for law and politics to begin remedying and rectifying the injustices and injuries they have suffered. Indeed, as Strakosch (2015, p. 133) concludes, "[t]here has never been a contradiction between the statement that Indigenous people deserve inclusion *by right* but must also be made to earn this inclusion *by qualification*." The qualification that earns indigenous peoples inclusion is and has been their subjugated position.

Thus, embedded in the idea of inclusion as a fix is a requirement that indigeneity has to uphold its vulnerability and 'injuredness'. The 'qualification' that indigeneity needs to fulfill in order to be recognized, and thus included, is dispossession. It is from this very position of being in need of or calling for protection that indigenous peoples have been allowed access to international political arenas. In the case of the UN, the peoples' demand that they be allowed into the organization was motivated by their lack of political voice and rights and the opportunity to gain international support for their domestic struggles. In Arctic politics, the protection demanded and received by the peoples has been an acknowledgment of their presence and stakeholdership in what was previously thought to be merely a natural environment devoid of a human presence. The inclusion of indigenous peoples in both of the forums is, however, an ongoing process, as the previously mentioned continuous processes of hearing and supporting the peoples demonstrate. Despite the allegedly equal footing of indigenous peoples in these forums, there is an ever-present need to develop their structures to make them more inclusive of indigenous peoples and their agendas. This implies that the Permanent Forum and the Arctic Council, as political bodies, also acknowledge that the peoples' full inclusion is still on its way. In the meanwhile, in order to eventually gain full-fledged political leverage and space, indigenous peoples are expected to demonstrate their rightful position as those in need of special inclusive and empowering measures.

While inclusion signifies recognition of the dispossession of indigenous peoples, it requires them to continue to make their case from the position of the dispossessed. The fact that politics, both in the UN and the Arctic Council, keeps returning to and assessing the implications of inclusion and the barriers to it makes it obvious that finding a single political 'fix' for the earlier, fundamental colonial exclusion is impossible. Instead, what international politics has done, and continues to do, to further the inclusion of indigenous peoples and their agendas in 'the most enabling way' is to carry out endless institutional assessments, structural adjustments and reorganization. While the stated aim of these measures is to improve the position of the peoples, they may in fact undermine the peoples' political and institutional position. Providing a variety of 'fixes' for the purpose of enhancing the peoples' position simultaneously requires them to demonstrate their marginalization, lack of political leverage and the ways in which the existing political system fails to support their cause. Indeed, at the very heart of political and legal recognition is the requirement that the indigenous peoples demonstrate their lack of resources: this is the impetus for law and politics to remedy victimization and otherness (Birrell 2016). In sum, the institutional and legal processes that seek to overcome and do away with dispossession paradoxically end up (re)producing and expecting the very otherness—dispossession, injury and vulnerability—they were designed to eradicate. This paradox applies in similar settings elsewhere on the globe: dispossessed people seeking recognition find themselves between a rock and a hard place.

If institutional inclusion has not been successful in remedying the situations of indigenous peoples, even less has it fulfilled its promise to alter the hierarchical ramifications of politics. As things stand, the prerequisite for gaining political recognition—and being included in structures built by those causing suffering in the first place—is that one lacks equal rights, has suffered injustices and, accordingly, is required to provide evidence of such suffering and deprivation. In this setting, as this book argues, the aim of international politics to remedy the dispossession of indigenous peoples by offering inclusion is, in fact, a continuation of the use of colonial power, for it places indigenous peoples in a position where they are never fully allowed to overcome their marginalization if they wish to gain the recognition that they rightfully demand. As a result, the discomfort being soothed and the unfavorable situation being remedied through these inclusive measures are those of the colonial states themselves.

Deceitful Inclusion

As part of the establishment of the UN Permanent Forum and the Arctic Council, what has provided the colonial states with peace of mind and signaled a response to the demands of indigenous peoples has been the idea of bringing states and indigenous peoples together around the same table. The often-voiced and acclaimed features of these forums are the irresistible invitation to indigenous peoples and states to 'sit at the same table', forge new types of 'partnerships' and enhance 'collaboration'. Institutional access, inclusion and partnership have become developments that one "cannot not want" (Butler and Athanasiou (2013, p. 76). To be sure, it is not a viable option for those who have been previously marginalized and excluded to refuse even a remote possibility of recognition and finally having a say in how they are, and will be, treated. Participation carries with it the possibility of change. As Butler and Athanasiou (2013, p. 76) note in the context of recognition, what one wants "is itself compelled by social and political categories, which means that such categories are not only objects of desire, but also historical conditions of desire." For indigenous peoples, participation is something that, given the historical conditions, they cannot do without.

However, political and institutional inclusion is deceitful. It is a politics of placation that operates, as Alfred (2005) puts it, through "surface reforms." This politics is a continuation of colonial practices, mentalities and rationalities of governing indigeneity. In Alfred's words,

> [...] surface reforms... are being offered precisely *because* they are useless to us [indigenous peoples] in the struggle to survive as peoples and so are no threat to the Settlers and... the people who control the Settler state. This is assimilation's end-game. (Alfred 2005, p. 37)

We find Alfred's critique of Canada as a settler state to be applicable to international politics as well. The promise of de-subjugation and gaining more leverage is, in actual fact and as discussed earlier, a move that dispossesses and hence does not mark a dissociation of colonial practices from this promise.

Indeed, inclusion as politics of placation is part and parcel of the neoliberal governance of indigeneity globally. The words by which this type of governance is described come to life in the work of the UN Permanent Forum and the Arctic Council, arenas that allegedly have been pioneers in the international community in (re)casting colonialism as a thing of the past. Colonial hierarchies, top-down control and brutal enforcement have been replaced by a neoliberal insistence on horizontal networking, negotiation, activation and stakeholder consensus in pursuit of a common end (Brown 2015, pp. 126–127). This "feel good" politics, as Ahmed (2012, p. 69) has named it, is seemingly inclusive of diversity. In effect, however, it works as an optical illusion that draws attention away from the unequal power dynamics embedded in the consensus-building and networking that both the UN Permanent Forum and the Arctic Council promote.

The UN Permanent Forum, for all its celebrated features that include the indigenous peoples and their agendas, is fraught with problematic issues when it comes to the peoples actually participating and affecting its policies. These range from practical issues such as the cost of travel to the mandate and power of the Forum. For example, to date the annual sessions of the

Forum have all been held at UN Headquarters in New York City. For most of the representatives of indigenous peoples traveling to New York and staying for the duration of the ten-day sessions become extremely expensive, many lack steady sources of funding, which prevents them from participating altogether.

The adoption of recommendations in the Permanent Forum is another critical issue. Recommendations of the Permanent Forum, among the outcomes of the annual sessions, are made by consensus. There is a great struggle against time here as well, for the UN conference services set deadlines by which the members of the Forum must prepare their recommendations in order for them to be copied and circulated in the six official UN languages. Due to the demand for reaching a consensus within strict time limits, the process of drafting the recommendations is often complicated (Handbook for Participants 2007). As a result, the requirement of consensus further serves to gloss over the variety of indigenous concerns, situations and demands.

The demand for consensus also has an impact on the work of the 16 expert members of the Permanent Forum. These experts, both indigenous- and state-nominated, are supposed to act in a personal capacity and not represent either particular indigenous peoples or states. Yet, there is no denying that they may have topics of special personal interest and differing worldviews. Accordingly, reaching a consensus requires not only that the indigenous-nominated experts agree on the issue at hand, but that they reach a consensus with the state-nominated experts. At the end of the day, the political leverage that indigenous peoples allegedly have in the Permanent Forum—leverage perceived as being achieved owing to equal footing between state and indigenous experts—becomes diluted through the requirement of consensus. Consensus is never more than a general, descriptive and all-round statement.

The Permanent Forum has also been criticized for being no more than a bureaucratic machine that churns out recommendations without proper follow-up. Responding to this criticism in recent years, the Forum has begun working in bi-annual cycles, with one year having a specific theme and the next focusing on reviewing implementation. Nevertheless, it remains rather unclear to what extent the recommendations of the Forum actually 'reach the ground' and translate into concrete actions.

The practical challenges of indigenous peoples' participation in the Arctic Council resemble those experienced in the UN Permanent Forum. Due to the rotating chairmanships and agendas of the Council, the combinations of representatives taking part in its work and meetings vary significantly, making strategic networking difficult among indigenous (and other) groups. The change in chairmanship and policy program every second year makes the work short-sighted. A geographical challenge is that the meetings take place in different locations around the Arctic, where distances are great and the means of travel often very limited and expensive. Combined with indigenous peoples' organizations having limited funds for traveling, this has meant that, despite the right to participate, representatives are often unable to attend meetings.

Due to the informal working practices of the Council and the broad scope of the themes taken up by its working groups, studies on the (potential) ways in which the new roles of agency accorded to the peoples in particular had or could have influenced Arctic politics are lacking (for a notable exception, see Sinevaara-Niskanen 2015). As the Council does not have a budget of its own, the projects conducted in its working groups depend on national funding and states' commitment to act as lead countries (Hønneland and Stokke 2007). Observers, who represent, for example, non-Arctic states and different types of governmental organizations, may also take part in suggesting and funding projects. The projects engage various researchers and experts who represent Arctic states and indigenous peoples and whose task is to produce and disseminate knowledge on development in the Arctic. Despite the Council having an established practice of operating through projects and the compilation of scientific reports, there is no particular procedure by which these activities are organized. The process by which researchers are invited to take part in projects and write reports may vary considerably. In the end, non-formal procedures and, for example, money, determine what issues are addressed within the Council's working groups. It is thus often unclear whether or to what extent indigenous representatives, largely lacking the funding to even take part in working group meetings, can influence the topics discussed.

On balance, the celebrated inclusion of indigenous peoples in the processes of the Council has not translated into greater diversity in the agendas. Indigenous issues—when considered—are still presented under a heading of their own and understood in a narrow and stereotypical way: it is not the indigenous representatives who frame projects as funders but mostly the states and their policies. Indigenous causes and agendas are understood as relating to traditional livelihoods, peoples' relationship to nature, community viability and cultural practices. The issues perceived as 'indigenous' differ significantly from those associated with development in the Arctic in general, driven as this is by large-scale political and environmental processes.

A vision of regional development to the effect that only local, traditional and environmental issues are relevant to indigenous peoples overlooks the implications for the peoples of that development (Sinevaara-Niskanen 2015).

Along with the UN Permanent Forum and the Arctic Council, the UNDRIP has been considered by many as signaling a change in international politics. Referred to as the most significant milestone in the recognition of indigenous peoples and their rights in international politics, the Declaration has been seen as proof that indigenous concerns have now been integrated into those of the international community at large. However, as the process of adopting the UNDRIP shows, this is far from the case. There were several Western, pro-human rights countries with large indigenous populations—Canada, the USA, Australia and New Zealand—that initially voted against adoption of the Declaration and in fact did not join the 144 member states that did adopt it at the UN General Assembly on 13 September 2007. Immediately after voting against the Declaration, these states faced diplomatic criticism for not joining the international consensus on the rights of indigenous peoples and were pressured by the indigenous peoples living within their borders. Over the course of 2009 and 2010, all four states changed their position on the Declaration, expressing their 'support' for or 'endorsement' of it (Lightfoot 2012, pp. 102–103). Lightfoot's (2012) critical analysis of this process shows that these late adopters of the UNDRIP engaged in a move of "selective endorsement" of the Declaration in order to preserve their pro-human rights image while maintaining their legal and political status quo. Although they eventually adopted the UNDRIP, they still have no intention of implementing it.

Like the other reforms mentioned above, the principle of free, prior and informed consent (FPIC) of indigenous peoples to the use of natural resources on their land is built on an idea that consensus can be reached. The principle has been outlined in the UNDRIP and in ILO Convention No. 169 (Gilbert and Doyle 2011). Negotiations on projects affecting indigenous lands proceed from the assumption that the worldviews of those meeting are sufficiently compatible to make an agreement possible. As some critical views have also noted (Cariño 2005), the peoples' perspectives are taken into account only in a form that can eventually produce consent. As its very name suggests, the principle is based on a consensus- and agreement-seeking mindset that precludes the possibility of disagreement and refusal. If the principle in itself already lays out the desired outcome of the related negotiations—the need for consent—it is worth asking to what extent 'freedom' describes the process. Furthermore, if freedom genuinely applied, should not the principle be called 'Free, Prior and Informed Decision', a wording that would allow refusal to be one outcome of the process?

The underlying logic of ILO Convention No. 169, which aims to safeguard the rights of indigenous peoples to land and participation in development processes, is no exception in its praise for consultation and participation. As Larsen (2016) has critically noted, the soft wording of the Convention, while suggesting greater involvement of the peoples, can be actually read as a continuation of assimilation. The way in which the Convention emphasizes, for example, the need for consultation and the aim of reaching consent, narrows down the range of claims available to the peoples as it leaves little room for genuine contestation that could potentially change the setting that has already been laid out. ILO 169 is continuation of the colonial mindset and its understanding of development. Amid these colonial ramifications, those in power (i.e. the market, states, development funders) are the ones to set the pace for development and those with less power—paradoxically the ones deemed to be in need of that development (e.g. indigenous peoples)—are merely to be consulted and invited to agree and give their consent to a course of development designed by others.

The establishment of the UN Permanent Forum and the Arctic Council and the inclusion of indigenous peoples in their work are political milestones that are visible and can be highlighted as events signaling that 'something has happened'. Likewise, packaging the rights of indigenous peoples into the UNDRIP can be offered as visible evidence that international politics is recognizing indigenous peoples and their rights. As noted, the adoption of the UNDRIP has been considered a significant legal milestone. It was the technical and bureaucratic culmination of what was a long saga in different UN processes. All of these are considered to prove that 'something is being done' in international politics and that indigenous concerns are being acknowledged. Indeed, what these processes of political and legal inclusion respond to is the need on the part of the colonial states to provide evidence enabling them to say that colonialism is over. The celebrated 'eventful-ness' of inclusion also makes visible the desire to think that there is a technical 'fix' to the wrongdoings of the past. It is a way of thinking, as Simpson (2016, p. 2) puts it, that allows one to say "'it is over' we are done with that, 'we' can now move on and thus, it never happened." Tellingly, for example, the wording of the apology of Australia to its indigenous peoples, delivered in 2008, suggests that the heinous acts of violence, discrimination and terror of colonialism are now things of the past. The events that are offered as evidence of the states' remorse, state apologies being one, project a future—"A future where... the *injustices of the past* must never, never happen again" (Apology to Australia's Indigenous Peoples 2008, emphasis added).

The inclusion of indigenous peoples, the adoption of international legal instruments, such as the UNDRIP and ILO Convention No. 169, and the overarching emphasis on partnership are tantamount to what Corntassel (2012) has defined as a "politics of distraction." This is a politics that, while performing grandiose political and legal acts and proclaiming commitment to progress, draws attention away from the continuing distortion of and inequality in the conditions of the peoples in many countries. In the midst of globally visible and high profile acts of politics of distraction, it seems convincing, even valid, to suggest that the progress to come will erase the injustices of the past.

Behind the momentous events that seem to break with a past of colonialism and exclusion is colonialists' guilt and desire for their own redemption. Inclusion offers one of the 'smoke screens' that enable international politics to look 'good', feel 'good' and seemingly to be doing 'good', all the while maintaining its original colonial pursuits. Inclusion helps temper indigenous voices that have accused politics, and rightly so, for colonizing and marginalizing them, and creates an illusion that the peoples' concerns are being addressed. As the examples of the UN Permanent Forum and the Arctic Council show, colonial constellations of power and political structures have not changed. It is well worth reflecting on whether the stated aim of inclusion has ever meant changing the disparity in power relations.

Sadly, it must be concluded that no such fundamental change was ever intended in the first place. International politics, with its particular power set-up and political structures, remains colonial. Inclusion is one of the gimmicks by which colonial guilt is assuaged and colonial practices continued. The benevolent events of 'progress' hide contemporary colonialism in plain view. Simpson's (2016) critique of settler states applies unequivocally in the case of international politics and its desire for inclusion. She notes that "[s]ettler colonialism appears in its non-appearance as a sturdy, structuring logic but also a shifting and impossible assemblage....what makes... able to treat something as a thing, as an event and then deny it ever happened, as it happens before your very eyes" (Simpson 2016, pp. 2–3). When 'good' things are finally happening and progress is right under your nose, it seems that their 'goodness' is insurmountably difficult to question. The inclusion of indigenous peoples has become a sacrament of international politics that promises salvation. The ideal of saving indigenous peoples, by having them included, recognized and granting them rights, is so precious that nobody even thinks to problematize it.

Partners in Crime

Often perceived as a departure from a past politics embedded in colonialism, inclusion and recognition seem to signal a change for the better in the ways in which indigeneity and international politics now mesh. However, with inclusion, colonialism can join hands with neoliberal governance. Offering indigenous peoples a separate 'slot' to participate, both in the UN Permanent Forum and the Arctic Council, their inclusion is a carefully choreographed move in which the balance and cost-effectiveness of power is meticulously calculated. Colonialism conducted in a neoliberal way, while assuming active agency on the part of indigenous peoples in its processes, does not seek or want to change the fundamental condition of the peoples, including the power setting of international politics in which they are embedded.

Indeed, a shift in politics to emphasizing partnership and cooperation is a signature move of the current neoliberal order. Not only is the active participation of indigenous peoples that is being called for but also that of other marginalized groups, such as refugees, the rural poor and communities whose existence is threatened by environmental changes (Appadurai 2002; Agrawal 2005; Li 2007; Duffield 2007). Neoliberal politics of development have promoted active agency, stakeholdership and empowerment of those who previously have not been considered to have any part in deciding the course of developments. The fundamental change in this mindset is that the world is "insecure by design" (Evans and Reid 2014), making active participation a necessity if one wants to safeguard oneself. In many cases, as critical development studies have shown, the call for participation has been directed specifically to those who have been marginalized. Paradoxically, then, the ones deprived of and in need of resources are also the ones who are required to draw on their (non-existing or meager) resources to overcome their dispossession. For indigenous peoples, in addition to actively participating in order to try to secure themselves in the present and the future, active participation is, and has been, a precondition for having past injustices addressed, negotiated and, potentially, dealt with. As the establishment of the UN bodies for indigenous issues, such as the Working Group on Indigenous Populations and, later, the Permanent

Forum, prove, the persistence of indigenous peoples has been vital for creating these political spaces. For indigenous peoples, who have been marginalized and have lacked any political security, the active involvement required in promoting their cause is not new as such, but the partnership and inclusion proffered by neoliberal politics are novel.

This current political modality of neoliberal governing is fluid and shifting in its means, but its rationality is driven by an economic logic (e.g. Larner 2000; Lemke 2012). In that rationality, 'economy', as Brown (2015, p. 62) points out, "signifies specific principles, metrics, and modes of conduct, including for endeavors where monetary profit and wealth are not at issue." Accordingly, the question of political inclusion does not remain untouched by the calculations of cost-effectiveness. States may have given up a share of the political authority that historically belonged to them exclusively, but this has been a very small price to pay. As Alfred (2005, p. 138) has also noted as part of his criticism of the policies of settler states, "[t]he token amounts of money given and limited minority-group rights granted to indigenous peoples" have been a bargain for the states wishing to redeem themselves from "the moral repercussions of conquest." Thus, the aim of global politics to make amends has involved evaluations of moral, political and economic 'profits' and 'costs'. Where inclusion is concerned, the profit for states and the international community at large has been to gain an image of promoting justice, progress and equality. The cost is that states can no longer autocratically decide on behalf of the peoples living in their territory without facing criticism, shame and pressure.

Tellingly, the way in which both the UN Permanent Forum and the Arctic Council accommodate indigenous participation has not threatened states' ultimate or factual power. In the case of the UN Permanent Forum, it became evident already during the establishment of the body that indigenous peoples wanted to have an equal position with states in it. The legitimacy of the Forum, in the eyes of indigenous peoples especially, was secured by insisting on this principle of state and indigenous representatives acting on an equal footing. As a result, states wanted to limit the decision-making powers of the Forum, even though indigenous peoples would have liked to see a body with decision-making power and more actual authority. One of the prices to pay for indigenous peoples' 'equal' inclusion was having a forum with a mere consultative role. Similarly, in the case of the Arctic Council, discussion of transforming the organization from one making non-binding decisions into one making binding decisions has revealed its essentially hierarchical nature. Criticism has pointed out that such an increase in the powers of the Council would mean a weakening of the position of indigenous peoples: in a weaker framework, where the Council has no more than a consultative role, the peoples' position is strong. It is in this vein that Hale (2005, p. 20) has pointed out that "indigenous 'representatives' accept recognition in exchange for compliance with the economic and political constraints that follow." At the end of the day, a gain in inclusion means a loss in power.

The political move from the colonialism of the past to the neoliberal present has meant a radical shift from ignoring indigenous peoples as inhabitants of states to singling the peoples out as groups responsible for representing themselves. The opportunity to take part in politics has translated into a responsibility and need to do so. Indigenous peoples are expected to transform their own conditions and to assume responsibility for managing risks. Rather than looking to international politics to provide protection and security, the neoliberal mindset requires subjects to "produce individually what was once provisioned in the common" (Brown 2015, p. 42), thus intensifying inequalities. Both in the case of the UN Permanent Forum and the Arctic Council, the leading idea is that indigenous people are to represent themselves—despite the fact that the states in which the peoples live are already represented in these forums. Here, the indigenous peoples constitute a special case, as states are ordinarily assumed to represent their inhabitants and their concerns, well-being and interests.

The fantasy of 'teamwork', 'partnership' and 'cooperation' is part of the neoliberal mindset. As the aim is to reach 'stakeholder consensus'—in the name of equality and inclusiveness but in fact to serve cost-effectiveness—individual interests and local claims become watered down and glossed over. The ways in which inclusion goes hand in hand with the demand for stakeholder consensus are reflected concretely in the constant struggle against time in the annual sessions of the UN Permanent Forum. As there are large numbers of indigenous organizations that want to speak on a specific agenda item in the plenary session, being there does not mean getting heard. For example, in the 2007 annual session, which included a discussion on eradicating poverty, 70 organizations expressed an interest in giving a statement in the two hours that was allocated to the subject. This being the case, the chair prefers collective statements of several participating organizations, often giving delegates delivering such statements a few minutes more than those of single organizations, who might get as little as three minutes to speak. The preference for collective statements translates into a loss of more nuanced indigenous concerns, placing, once again, the demand upon indigeneity to perform a coherent 'we'. In contrast, representatives of states are allowed more time and are less frequently interrupted, which speaks volumes about the still hierarchical nature of this arena (Lindroth 2011).

Indeed, the efficacy of "neoliberal multiculturalism," as Hale (2005, p. 13) observes, relies on the ability of those in power, to "restructure the arena of political contention"—the arena that could potentially function as a platform for the marginalized to gain rights and genuine political influence. The inclusion of indigenous peoples in international politics has not meant a diminishing of state control even though this might appear to be the case in light of the new types of 'partnership' and 'cooperation' that are being promoted. For indigenous peoples, states' control, coupled with the market logic proffered by the prevailing neoliberal rationality, as well as its call for active participation, has meant losing once and for all any "guarantees of protection by the liberal state" (Brown 2015, p. 64). A salient example is found in the Australian context, where Strakosch (2015) has examined the withdrawal of politics from the visible spaces of national politics and the distribution of responsibility to the fringes of decentralized regional and communal programs. In both national and international politics, the political, economic and social responsibility for improving conditions has been placed squarely on the shoulders of those who lack protection afforded by rights, well-being, security or political representation.

Policing Indigeneity

The institutional, observable and technical reforms undertaken in international politics to include indigenous peoples have been made with the 'good' of the peoples in mind. The benevolent will to include masks the less heartening side of the partnership, cooperation and involvement proffered. In effect, the reforms are part of the array of neoliberal tactics used by colonial power today. As the reforms convey an image that actual changes are taking place, they are also conveniently available to the international political community as evidence in defending itself against any criticism that it has excluded and marginalized the peoples.

Inclusion as an invitation to sit down around the same table defuses the challenge that indigenous peoples pose to states and international politics. By being included in the political system of those who have colonized them, the peoples and their causes have been made partners in a politics that has, in fact, never abandoned its hierarchical and unequal premises. The seeming 'goodness' of inclusion has sheltered the illegitimacy of the physical, legal and political bases of the current order from being exposed and attacked. Having ready evidence of indigenous inclusion and being able to appeal to this act of 'doing good' have enabled the states to dismiss the fundamental basis of any statements that colonialist mentalities persist.

What benevolent inclusion does not impact is the underlying premise of injustice in the relationship between the injured and their protector. Like many of the colonial interventions of the past, the political inclusion of indigenous peoples in global politics today has been based on the principle of protection and 'doing good'. The celebration of institutional inclusion that has taken place in the UN Permanent Forum and Arctic Council is built on an awareness that the peoples and their causes are in need of attention and special measures. Indeed, the peoples themselves have been active in voicing their needs and pointing out the lack of safeguards for their political position. The inclusion of indigenous peoples is a matter of recognizing the peoples. At the same time, however, it is misrecognition, for it unceasingly requires the peoples to uphold their position as vulnerable subjects if they are to be deemed worthy of the political position gained.

Alfred (2005, p. 130) has called this (mis)recognition the 'menu' of identities and cultural choices that is presented to indigenous peoples by those who offer them 'a seat at the same table'. Similarly, Povinelli (2011, p. 31) has noted that "the subjects of recognition are called to present difference in a form that feels like difference, but does not permit any real difference to confront a normative world." The ways in which indigeneity becomes recognized are the polar opposite of what the western, so-called developed, industrial world is considered to be. Indigeneity is called for as the vulnerable one, the one who is injured, lacerated and in need of protection. In this role, indigeneity is always the Other and a rung lower in the hierarchy.

In addition to inclusion (mis)recognizing indigeneity and its difference from the outset, the mechanical, institutional and administrative inclusion that desires partnership and 'sitting at the same table' blunts political action. The neoliberal drive to include and the expectation that indigeneity as the Other is somehow homogeneous entail the idea that consensus, not contest, is what is sought. But, as Brown (2015, p. 127, see also Strakosch 2015) has concluded, the neoliberal ethos of cooperation "eliminates politics, conflict, and deliberation about common values and ends." Through inclusion, the contestation that is arguably the essence of politics is avoided, and the indigenous cause is reduced to the most easily reachable common denominator. This is especially the case in the UN Permanent Forum and the Arctic Council, which are hyped as the premier platforms for cooperation, but have no more than a consultative role. Even the ways in which the inclusion of indigenous peoples in these forums is structured and implemented indicate that the people face severe challenges in contesting, altering and questioning the very premises of the content and workings of the politics. In this respect, inclusion marks a narrowing of the political in indigeneity.

Within this frame, rather than enabling political action, the will to include constitutes a policing move targeting indigeneity. As we have pointed out earlier in this chapter, inclusion is not, if it ever was, an effort to correct wrongdoings or improve conditions but to ensure and maintain a grip on indigeneity. In other words, the price to pay for institutional inclusion and recognition is that indigeneity—as a difference marked by vulnerability and injuredness—becomes policed. Inclusion is thus a move that sustains dispossession.

Inclusion and recognition are the ways in which the policing of indigeneity becomes possible. In order to even start thinking about changing conditions and gaining redress, indigenous peoples have had to demand recognition of the wrongdoings perpetrated against them. What makes the quest for recognition irresistible is its promise of change, which would otherwise be impossible. At the precise moment of starting the quest for recognition, indigeneity enters a 'limbo' that is no longer about changing and correcting the injustices of the past but about indigeneity becoming defined by its being injured. Indeed, as Butler and Athanasiou (2013, p. 87) note, the current political framework is obsessed with the identity that is injured rather than the condition within which those with that identity live:

> There is a difference between calling for recognition of oppression in order to overcome oppression and calling for recognition of identity that now becomes defined by its injury. The problem with the latter is that it inscribes injury into identity and makes that into a presupposition of political self-representation. As such, injury cannot be recast as an oppression to be overcome.

In many cases, indigenous peoples have not had any other viable choice than to seek political and legal recognition. The current neoliberal politics has also made indigenous peoples complicit in the desire for inclusion. This all means that indigenous peoples are trapped in a vicious cycle where they are expected to re-represent their injury in order to gain the recognition that is a necessary precondition for them to get justice. Even if the peoples should demand recognition of the oppression that has taken place, the politics of inclusion only recognizes the subject that is oppressed. Where the indigenous peoples are concerned, politics is no longer a matter of changing circumstances but of indigeneity itself. What is being pursued is indigeneity as a particular type of subjectivity that must reproduce, alter and adapt itself to given political conditions. In the process, neoliberal partnership and empowerment shift the burden of responsibility for improving the indigenous peoples' lives onto the peoples themselves. While recognition promises a subject 'a place at the table' and equal rights—rights that are difficult not to want—no pursuit of recognition can ever transform the machinery within which the subject seeks that recognition.

References

Agrawal, Arun. 2005. *Environmentality. Technologies of Government and the Making of Subjects*. Durham: Duke University Press.

Ahmed, Sara. 2012. *On Being Included: Racism and Diversity in Institutional Life*. Durham: Duke University Press.

Alfred, Taiaiake. 2005. *Wasáse: Indigenous Pathways of Action and Freedom*. Peterborough: Broadview Press.

Apology to Australia's Indigenous Peoples. 2008. http://www.australia.gov.au/about-australia/our-country/our-people/apology-to-australias-indigenous-peoples. Accessed 16 Apr 2017.

Appadurai, Arjun. 2002. Deep Democracy: Urban Governmentality and the Horizon of Politics. *Public Culture* 14 (1): 21–47.

Arctic Human Development Report. 2004. Akyreyri: Stefansson Arctic Institute.

Axworthy, Timothy S., Timo Koivurova, and Waliul Hasanat, eds. 2012. *The Arctic Council: Its Place in the Future of Arctic Governance*. Toronto: Walter & Duncan Gordon Foundation.

Birrell, Kathleen. 2010. 'An Essential Ghost': Indigeneity Within the Legal Archive. *The Australian Feminist Law Journal* 33 (1): 81–99.

———. 2016. *Indigeneity: Before and Beyond the Law*. Abingdon: Routledge.

Brown, Wendy. 2015. *Undoing the Demos: Neoliberalism's Stealth Revolution*. New York: Zone Books.

Butler, Judith, and Athena Athanasiou. 2013. *Dispossession: The Performative in the Political*. Cambridge: Polity Press.

Cariño, Joji. 2005. Indigenous Peoples' Right to Free, Prior, Informed Consent: Reflections on Concepts and Practice. *Arizona Journal of International and Comparative Law* 22 (1): 19–39.

Cobo Report. 1983. Study of the Problem of Discrimination Against Indigenous Populations. UN Doc. E/CN.4/Sub.2/1986/7 and Add. 1–4). Final Report Submitted by the Special Rapporteur, Mr. José Martínez Cobo. https://www.un.org/development/desa/indigenouspeoples/publications/2014/09/martinez-cobo-study/. Accessed 4 June 2017.

Corntassel, Jeff. 2008. Toward Sustainable Self-Determination: Rethinking the Contemporary Indigenous-Rights Discourse. *Alternatives* 33: 105–132.

———. 2012. Re-envisioning Resurgence. Indigenous Pathways to Decolonization and Sustainable Self-Determination. *Decolonization: Indigeneity, Education & Society* 1 (1): 86–101.

Dahl, Jens. 2012. *The Indigenous Space and Marginalized Peoples in the United Nations*. New York: Palgrave Macmillan.

Duffield, Mark. 2007. *Development, Security and Unending War. Governing the World of Peoples*. Cambridge: Polity Press.

Evans, Brad, and Julian Reid. 2014. *Resilient Life: The Art of Living Dangerously*. Cambridge: Polity Press.

Finland's Chairmanship Program 2017–2019. 2017. Finland's Chairmanship Program for the Arctic Council 2017–2019. http://www.arctic-council.org/images/PDF_attachments/FIN_Chairmanship/Finnish_Chairmanship_Program_Arctic_Council_2017-2019.pdf. Accessed 28 May 2017.

García-Alix, Lola. 2003. *The Permanent Forum on Indigenous Issues*. Copenhagen: IWGIA.

Gilbert, Jérémie, and Cathal Doyle. 2011. A New Dawn over the Land: Shedding Light on Collective Ownership and Consent. In *Reflections on the UN Declaration on the Rights of Indigenous Peoples*, ed. Stephen Allen and Alexandra Xanthaki, 289–328. Oxford: Hart Publishing.

Hale, Charles R. 2005. Neoliberal Multiculturalism: The Remaking of Cultural Rights and Racial Dominance in Central America. *PoLAR: Political and Legal Anthropology Review* 28 (1): 10–28.

Handbook for Participants. 2007. United Nations Permanent Forum on Indigenous Issues. http://www.un.org/esa/socdev/unpfii/documents/guide_participants_en.pdf. Accessed 19 June 2017.

Hønneland, Geir, and Olav Schram Stokke, eds. 2007. *International Cooperation and Arctic Governance. Regime Effectiveness and Northern Region Building*. New York: Routledge.

Larner, Wendy. 2000. Neo-liberalism: Policy, Ideology, Governmentality. *Studies in Political Economy* 63: 5–25.

Larsen, Peter Bille. 2016. The 'New Jungle Law': Development, Indigenous Rights and ILO Convention 169 in Latin America. *International Development Policy* 7(1). https://poldev.revues.org/2220. Accessed 4 July 2017.

Lemke, Thomas. 2012. *Foucault, Governmentality, and Critique*. Boulder: Paradigm Publishers.

Li, Tania Murray. 2007. *The Will to Improve: Governmentality, Development, and the Practice of Politics.* Durham: Duke University Press.

Lightfoot, Sheryl. 2012. Selective Endorsement without Intent to Implement: Indigenous Rights and the Anglosphere. *The International Journal of Human Rights* 16 (1): 100–122.

Lindroth, Marjo. 2011. Paradoxes of Power: Indigenous Peoples in the Permanent Forum. *Cooperation and Conflict* 46 (4): 542–561.

Lindroth, Marjo, and Heidi Sinevaara-Niskanen. 2013. At the Crossroads of Autonomy and Essentialism: Indigenous Peoples in International Environmental Politics. *International Political Sociology* 7 (3): 275–293.

Morgan, Rhiannon. 2011. *Transforming Law and Institution: Indigenous Peoples, the United Nations and Human Rights.* Farnham: Ashgate.

Niezen, Ronald. 2003. *The Origins of Indigenism: Human Rights and the Politics of Identity.* Berkeley: University of California Press.

Office of the United Nations High Commissioner for Human Rights. 2017a. Special Rapporteur on the Rights of Indigenous Peoples. http://www.ohchr.org/EN/Issues/IPeoples/SRIndigenousPeoples/Pages/SRIPeoplesIndex.aspx. Accessed 4 June 2017.

———. 2017b. Expert Mechanism on the Rights of Peoples. http://www.ohchr.org/EN/Issues/IPeoples/EMRIP/Pages/EMRIPIndex.aspx. Accessed 4 June 2017.

Povinelli, Elizabeth A. 2011. *Economies of Abandonment: Social Belonging and Endurance in Late Liberalism.* Durham: Duke University Press.

Simpson, Audra. 2016. Whither Settler Colonialism? *Settler Colonial Studies* 6 (4): 438–445.

Sinevaara-Niskanen, Heidi. 2015. *Setting the Stage for Arctic Development: Politics of Knowledge and the Power of Presence.* Rovaniemi: Lapland University Press.

Søvndahl Petersen, Tove. 1999. Preface to *The Permanent Forum on for Indigenous Peoples: The Struggle for a New Partnership,* ed. Lola García-Alix, pp. 8–11. Copenhagen: IWGIA. http://www.iwgia.org/iwgia_files_publications_files/0135_PermanentForum.pdf. Accessed 30 June 2017.

Stokke, Olav Schram. 2007. Examining the Consequences of Arctic Institutions. In *International Cooperation and Arctic Governance. Regime Effectiveness and Northern Region Building,* ed. Olav Schram Stokke and Geir Hønneland, 12–26. New York: Routledge.

Strakosch, Elizabeth. 2015. *Neoliberal Indigenous Policy: Settler Colonialism and the 'Post-Welfare' State.* London: Palgrave Macmillan.

UN Division for Social Policy and Development. 2017. News: Permanent Forum Concludes with Call to Action and Report. https://www.un.org/development/desa/indigenouspeoples/news/2017/05/un-permanent-forum-on-indigenous-issues-concludes-with-call-to-action/. Accessed 4 June 2017.

UN Letter of Invitation for Indigenous Peoples. 2016. Invitation to the Informal Launch Brief on the Next Steps of the Consultation on the Participation of Indigenous Peoples' Representatives and Institutions in Relevant United Nations Meetings on Issues Affecting Them. https://www.un.org/development/desa/indigenouspeoples/wp-content/uploads/sites/19/2016/09/Invitation-to-the-First-Informal-Briefing-28-09-16.pdf. Accessed 30 May 2017.

Wiessner, Siegfried. 2009. United Nations Declaration on the Rights of Indigenous Peoples. United Nations Audiovisual Library of International Law. http://legal.un.org/avl/pdf/ha/ga_61-295/ga_61-295_e.pdf. Accessed 19 June 2017.

CHAPTER 3

Vulnerable Yet Adaptive: Indigeneity in the Making

Qualifications for Entry

As discussed in the previous chapter, historical injury has been the precondition both for indigenous peoples to argue for entry into global politics and for that politics to recognize them. While an assumption of the peoples being vulnerable subjects prevails in international politics and its practices, as well as in the parlance and rationales of inclusion, politics today has changed and, with that, what is expected of indigenous representatives has gained new nuances. The scope of issues tackled in international politics has expanded extensively in the 20 years that indigenous peoples have been engaged in that politics, the UN Permanent Forum and the Arctic Council being prime examples. The politics that the peoples first encountered upon joining the UN Working Group on Indigenous Populations and the Arctic Council is very different than that seen today. The issues dealt with in relation to indigenous peoples in the UN and Arctic politics now range from global environmental degradation and large-scale questions of the use of natural resources to the changing living conditions of remote communities and the capacities of individuals to cope with drastic environmental, economic, political and social changes. Moreover, there is now much more information on the situation and well-being of indigenous peoples both nationally and internationally. At the same time, indigenous peoples are better aware of the circumstances of their counterparts around the globe and may assess their particular situation in this light.

M. Lindroth, H. Sinevaara-Niskanen, *Global Politics and Its Violent Care for Indigeneity*,
https://doi.org/10.1007/978-3-319-60982-9_3

Clearly, the institutional inclusion of indigenous peoples has produced more knowledge and awareness as well as enabled previously unthinkable collaboration and coalitions. This has been beneficial for the peoples; they have been able to attract international attention to and concern over their causes more effectively and to forge global cooperation among themselves and with states. Despite the practical challenges indigenous peoples face in participating in the meetings of the UN Permanent Forum and the Arctic Council, these forums have provided a physical platform for the peoples to meet one another. The challenges, as discussed in the previous chapter, include the expense of traveling to the locations where the meetings take place and the limited time allocated for presenting concerns. The coalitions formed and strengthened in the UN have been beneficial in the Arctic Council and vice versa. For example, the Saami Council, the international body for cooperation between the Saami peoples in Sweden, Norway, Finland and Russia, has played a prominent role in both the Arctic Council and the UN. Representatives of the Saami Council have played leading roles as chairs of the UN Permanent Forum (Lindroth 2006) and as trailblazers in shaping the status of Permanent Participants in the Arctic Council (Tennberg 1998).

The newly gained knowledge and forms of cooperation have not, however, erased indigenous peoples' need to justify their presence and cause in the eyes of global politics. The position of being injured, while still highly relevant for the peoples in their struggles for political and legal recognition, has morphed from a vulnerability to be eradicated into a vulnerability that in fact defines the peoples and that global politics can help them to cope with. The role of indigeneity as a permanently vulnerable state has been coupled with new expectations for indigenous peoples, expectations that stem from fundamental changes globally in the environment, the economy and politics. If the peoples' injuries, caused by a brutal past, were once the condition for them to enter international politics, their ability to contribute to global struggles in the midst of change is now the condition for entry and inclusion.

The new 'codes of entry' allowing indigenous peoples to argue for the validity of their role and cause in international politics are entangled with three perceived characteristics: their connectedness to the environment—and thus its changes—their historical and current vulnerability and, paradoxically, their ability to adapt. It is these three traits that validate the peoples as representatives in international politics, that qualify them, as it were. The positioning of indigenous peoples' political role in relation to these attributes is universally shared. The rhetoric, practices and products of both the UN Permanent Forum and the Arctic Council reflect the prevailing expectation, assumption and requirement that indigenous peoples represent these attributes. As this chapter will demonstrate, quite astonishingly, essentially identical wording is used in both of these separate political arenas—by both the states and indigenous peoples—when describing the role and significance of the peoples in statements, reports and policy documents.

The peoples' relationship to the environment, vulnerability in the face of past and current events and celebrated ability to adapt and survive—given their harsh past and prospect of an equally harsh future—form the qualifications that indigeneity must show proof of in contemporary global politics. The tropes of power embedded in the contemporary, seemingly well-meaning political inclusion, become discernible when these expected qualifications are subjected to critical scrutiny. The desire on the part of global politics to define and include indigeneity on the basis of these particular attributes is an ever-tightening grip on indigeneity. This new set of qualifications will not be the last, however, as the power of global politics that works through inclusion lies in its constantly creating new sets of criteria for the peoples to fulfill.

Bound to the Environment

The rise of environmental concerns and indigenous peoples' (alleged) close relationship to nature has been the principal reason for the inclusion of the peoples in the forums where contemporary international politics is carried on. Indigenous peoples have become representations and representatives of climate change (Martello 2008). They are perceived as living close to nature, having exclusive knowledge of the environment, making crucial observations of environmental changes and, thus, as having a special stewardship role toward the planet. In this capacity, they are viewed as valuable partners.

The environment has become a marker of sorts determining what indigenous peoples and their causes are expected to be. In many cases, the environment is relevant to indigenous peoples, as they have been pushed to the margins, to the edge of the world as it were. For example, indigenous peoples living in the Arctic must confront consequences of climate change whose severity is disproportionate in relation to the peoples' contribution to that change. The profound impacts on their living conditions and livelihoods include erosion, trans-boundary pollution and the melting of glaciers and permafrost (e.g. Sejersen 2015; Arctic Human Development Report 2015). While this is reality for many peoples, the presumption that all indigenous peoples live close to nature does not reflect the full spectrum of their lived realities. Urbanization is a global phenomenon that has affected the lives of indigenous communities every bit as much as it has those of other rural and remote communities in both developed and developing countries.

The connectedness of indigenous peoples to the environment has been acknowledged in international politics. In the case of the Arctic Council, the motive in doing so has been to gain regional environmental knowledge and the institutional accommodation of indigenous peoples and their particular knowledge. To a great extent, indigenous representatives are expected to provide that specific environmental knowledge for the benefit of the whole Arctic region. In the UN, the original idea of inclusion, based on human rights perspectives and providing political space for the mistreated, has been augmented by the growing attention to the ecological prowess of indigenous peoples. The prevailing idea is that indigenous peoples, with their intimate connections to the land, are able to offer crucial information on environmental changes and have the potential to help the rest of the world tackle these successfully.

The fundamental premise that indigenous peoples 'live their environment', have 'intimate knowledge of the climate' and possess 'special environmental knowledge' constitutes a set of criteria for indigenous participation. The assumption that indigenous peoples represent certain causes in global politics is very explicit. For example, the Arctic Climate Impact Assessment notes that indigenous peoples "live in the region all year round, have intimate knowledge of the land, sea, and climate" and that "[t]hey are an invaluable resource and important partners in research" and "demonstrate extensive knowledge about climate change in their daily lives" (Arctic Climate Impact Assessment 2005, p. 77, 81). Similarly, the final report of the annual session of the UN Permanent Forum from 2008 acknowledges the contribution that indigenous peoples can make in the struggle against climate change because of their traditional knowledge (Permanent Forum on Indigenous Issues 2008).

Indigeneity has become defined by the environmental conditions under which indigenous peoples live and an assumption that they enjoy a special relationship with their environment. At the same time, the political inclusion of the peoples has started to forcefully resonate with the growing global concern for the environment. The indigenous subject—included on the basis of its injuries—is now called upon and placed on a pedestal as one that can tell the rest of world how to live, survive and cope with changing surroundings. In our view, this transition in the position of indigenous peoples is a telltale sign of the continuous policing of indigeneity in international politics. The way in which the environment and environmental knowledge has become conditions of approval for the whole political existence of the peoples makes visible how indigeneity continues to be a target of colonial techniques of governing.

No one can escape being governed, but in the case of indigenous peoples, this governing is of particular kind. This particularity stems from the unfinished business of the colonial past, which from the very outset placed, and continues to place, the peoples physically, mentally and socially in the margins of societies and history. As targets of neoliberal governing, which urges one to 'educate' and 'empower' oneself and to exercise 'active citizenship' (e.g. Agrawal 2005; Li 2007), indigenous peoples are, however, in a different position than non-indigenous citizens. For example, in settler states, such as Australia, Canada and the USA, the conditions from which indigenous peoples are to lift themselves up are far more challenging and fundamentally complex (Statistics Canada 2006; Sutton 2009; Rosay 2016). It follows from the colonial past and its unfinished business that there are fundamental hierarchical differences in society and politics at large. The ways in which indigenous peoples are governed are particularly violent, due to not only the peoples being placed in the lowest ranks of the colonial hierarchy but also the absence of real attempts and a genuine desire to break that hierarchy. As our discussion in the previous chapter on deceitful inclusion shows, the wrongdoings of the past and present are yet to be properly addressed and the colonial patterns that cause them yet to be abolished.

The current politics of inclusion in the UN and the Arctic Council, if not recognizing the full scope of the challenges experienced by indigenous peoples, acknowledges the peoples' environmental stakeholdership; the peoples deserve and should be listened to based on their particular knowledge. The position of stakeholder is built upon the expectation of hierarchical otherness. The particular knowledge that indigenous peoples are assumed to represent and that is sought-after is remote, rural and local knowledge. The 'remoteness' of indigenous peoples' knowledge legitimizes their status as valid participants in international politics. Belonging to a community affected by environmental problems gives the peoples an entitlement and a right to speak. What results is "eco-indigenism," as Sissons (2005) calls it, a mindset that confines indigeneity to being nothing more than a matter of the environment and saving the nature. The logic of gaining recognition by providing evidence of one's dispossession, seen in the previous chapter, where inclusion was secured by dint of injury, would seem to prevail in the case of environmental issues as well: indigeneity enters international politics as a subjectivity that is bound to its degrading environmental conditions.

The special knowledge that indigenous peoples are said to possess is referred to as 'traditional (ecological) knowledge'. Traditional knowledge is revered as a counterweight to Western scientific knowledge and its failed efforts to understand the complexity of ecosystems and their changes (e.g. Heinämäki 2009). Even though traditional knowledge is welcomed, a problematic relationship between different kinds of knowledges prevails. There is still a gap between the formalized knowledges of science and the local understandings generated in the course of everyday life. Even though indigenous peoples are taken into international politics to represent traditional knowledge and, in some cases, even considered sources from whom the world can learn how to co-exist with the environment, the hierarchy between the different kinds of knowledges positions indigenous knowledge as irrational and anecdotal (Watson 2015). While belonging to the category of environmental subjects enables indigenous peoples to enter international politics, it does not necessarily translate into their being heard in that forum. Due to the colonial past, the inclusion of indigenous peoples on the basis of their traditional knowledge is also problematic, as much of that knowledge has been a target of eradication. If such knowledge existed but was then lost as a consequence of colonialism, how is it justified and fair to demand such knowledge of the peoples now? Once again, indigenous peoples need to earn their status in international politics.

Vulnerability Validates

The defining element in the acknowledged relation between indigeneity and the environment is vulnerability. In the environmental and human rights debates, indigenous peoples are frequently defined as groups at risk and in need of having their vulnerability recognized. In the context of the Permanent Forum, it has been stated that indigenous peoples have special knowledge which has to be validated (Laub 2008). Similarly, in the Arctic, it has been said that local voices in the remote regions are often not heard even though they should be (Arctic Climate Impact Assessment 2005, p. 87). The underlying logic is that indigenous peoples are custodians of nature because of their close relationship with their environment and, in particular, their nature-based livelihoods (e.g. Smith 2007; Martello 2008). Owing to this close relationship, they are vulnerable to environmental changes and thus should be considered important actors in environmental politics.

Phrases that are often heard in the UN emphasize how, for indigenous peoples climate change is "a matter of life and death" (Fiu Mataese Elisara 2008), "may threaten [their] very existence" (Briceño 2008) and is "putting [our] survival as peoples at risk" (Bastidas 2008). Due to climate change, "indigenous peoples live in ecosystems at serious risk from degradation" (Olsson 2008). The peoples are "disproportionally affected by climate change" (Djonkou 2008) since they are those "least responsible" for causing climate change but those "most affected" (Olsson 2008) by its consequences. Indeed, the common manner of presenting indigeneity is in terms of risks and threats. The image of victims has also been appropriated by indigenous peoples themselves. Their lives are considered 'particularly and immediately threatened' and, as the UN rhetoric describes it, they are 'the poorest of the poor' and the 'most marginalized'.

The current international political inclusion of indigenous peoples and the concern for indigeneity stem from the peoples' role as (local) vulnerable populations. Due to their vulnerable position, indigenous peoples are viewed not only as knowledge-holders but also, and most importantly, as stakeholders who experience and observe the environment in their daily lives. This perception is reflected in the following excerpt from the Arctic Climate Impact Assessment:

> Within the context of climate change, indigenous observations and perspectives offer great insights not only in terms of the nature and extent of environmental change, but also in terms of the significance of such change for those peoples whose cultures are built on an intimate connection with the arctic landscape. (Arctic Climate Impact Assessment 2005, p. 62)

Environmental issues and the concomitant discussion of vulnerability show the ways in which the presence of indigenous peoples in international politics has changed. In the very beginning of the peoples' involvement in the UN, in the 1970s, their position as vulnerable claimants validated their access. The aim of the UN was to give them a voice and a say in issues that concerned them in order to extricate them from their marginalized condition. The people's vulnerability had to be erased. Now, with the world facing environmental threats whose scope is beyond anyone's ability to grasp, the vulnerability of indigenous peoples has ceased being an issue to resolve. On the contrary, vulnerability to environmental changes has become an attribute that validates the peoples' expertise, knowledge and stakeholdership. Their vulnerability validates their involvement as it is seen as entailing particular expertise and powers of observation that can potentially help humankind at large (Permanent Forum on Indigenous Issues 2008).

According to Fineman (2013), vulnerability is a universal condition of human beings. However, critical scholars, in their analysis of contemporary politics, have noted that vulnerability is not a universally shared experience (e.g. Evans and Reid 2014). It is a condition only presumed of and assigned to some. In our view, vulnerability is one of the particular premises that lays a claim on indigeneity in international politics. Indigeneity is acknowledged, but that recognition is partial and selective as it marks indigeneity as bound to its environment and to the injuries caused by changes in it. "Ecological ethnicity" (Parajuli 2004, p. 150) becomes indigenous identity. What one might consider benevolent acknowledgment has actually turned out to set criteria for authenticity. Especially where ecological discussions are concerned, this requirement of 'authenticity' is, as Sissons (2005) has critically argued, oppressive. Indigenous peoples need to perform their vulnerability in order to be considered 'authentic' in the eyes of international politics. However, the position of being the 'most severely affected' local stakeholder who has environmental observations to offer, drastically, limits the range of issues and topics that the peoples can legitimately raise and discuss.

In the UN and Arctic politics, the concern for the vulnerability of indigenous peoples has translated into inclusion and a welcoming of the peoples. The well-meaning aim has been that institutional inclusion would offset vulnerability and that such inclusion would be an 'asset' for both indigenous peoples and international politics. However, as we have argued earlier, the mere existence of the UN Permanent Forum and the Arctic Council has not diminished the vulnerability of the peoples. The formal state-based structures of these international political forums have been built on the basis of manufactured vulnerabilities of indigenous peoples, vulnerabilities that are politically commissioned from the peoples at particular times by international politics. Whether indigenous peoples accept this premise or not, it is vulnerability that politics draws on and exploits. What the UN and the Arctic Council commission from the peoples today is local environmental subjectivity.

Politically, vulnerability is used to bring into being and 'foretell' a specific indigeneity. Indigenous peoples are addressed as a particular target group, one that is helpless and in need of support. Instead of providing indigenous peoples with real leverage, the emphasis on vulnerability portrays them, yet again, as objects of something that is already taking place or about to happen. As subjects deemed perpetually vulnerable, they are positioned merely to react and accommodate themselves, once again, to inevitable future changes. The mentality goes hand in hand with the neoliberal idea of the world as insecure, where vulnerability is a "defining condition of existence" (Furedi 2008, p. 652; see also Reid 2012). The inclusion of indigenous peoples in international politics on the basis of their vulnerability has been a strategic move. Invoking the peoples' marginalization, victimization and injury—conditions that render them vulnerable—has in effect, cemented indigeneity as permanent state of vulnerability. The global politics of today, instead of according more political space and power, executes maneuvers of institutional inclusion that facilitate imposing particular requirements on indigeneity, vulnerability being an enduring one.

Adaptation Glorifies

Along with the emphasis on vulnerability, there is hype surrounding adaptation in international politics dealing with the current global changes and the ways in which the vulnerable indigenous subject is positioned in relation to them. Environmental changes have had profound effects on the conditions of life and living, bringing changes in livelihoods, eradicating living space and causing ecological disasters to which the human race must adapt. Indigenous peoples are portrayed as prime examples of adaptation due to their demonstrated ability to persevere despite colonial practices and to survive in the face of profound risks to their environments. Adaptation is also embraced by indigenous peoples as proof of their ability to resist and persist as peoples under extreme pressure.

International politics in the UN Permanent Forum and the Arctic Council is shot through with adaptation rhetoric. Assumptions and expectations that indigenous peoples must, can and will adapt are clearly stated in both of these forums. The Arctic Climate Impact Assessment, for example, notes the continuous need of indigenous peoples to adapt:

> The challenge posed by climate change to indigenous peoples is their ability to respond and adapt to changes in the local environment, while continuing to prosper. Since the history of indigenous peoples is replete with change, it is important to ask whether they and their cultures are threatened by continued change, or whether change is just a threat to current understanding of the environment, which in any case is continually changing, slowly and on a daily basis. (Arctic Climate Impact Assessment 2005. p. 76)

The discussions of the Permanent Forum also highlight the role of indigenous peoples, in the face of environmental changes, as valuable partners in and contributors to global efforts to adapt. As the indigenous chairperson of the 2008 Permanent Forum stated, indigenous peoples "can significantly contribute to designing and implementing more appropriate and sustainable mitigation and adaptation measures" (Tauli-Corpus 2008).

Indigenous peoples' ability to constantly adapt is not confined to the environment but rather extends to all spheres of social life, such as the economy, politics and law. The Arctic Human Development Report illustrates the common ground in international politics reflecting how indigenous peoples as representatives of 'remote' Arctic societies are viewed:

> Nor is climate change the only threat to Arctic societies and cultures. On the contrary, there is also a growing need to respond effectively to fast changes in economic, legal, and political systems as well as to changes in other biophysical systems. To meet this challenge, Arctic societies will have to balance the retention of longstanding social practices with the introduction of new forms of knowledge and innovative technologies or, in other words, find the right mix of continuity and change. (Arctic Human Development Report 2004, pp. 230–231)

As local vulnerable groups, the peoples must live under simultaneous expectations of responsiveness and flexibility. The requirement for indigeneity to accommodate itself to change is inescapable.

Discussion on the environment, in particular, makes visible how indigenous peoples need to adapt and accommodate to changes that are very much present in their communities even though they have not brought these about themselves. The need to adapt and to 'bounce back' makes indigenous peoples responsible for coping and persisting in the face of challenges. More importantly, adaptation has come to embody the essence of what the world wants indigeneity to be. The political celebration of adaptive indigeneity also manifests itself in the institutional arrangements of 'adding' indigenous peoples and 'stirring'. Rather than giving indigenous peoples a stronger political position and opportunities to exert influence, this seeming inclusion suggests that it is not the current politics that needs to adjust itself, but rather indigeneity that needs to stretch to fit that politics and its consequences.

As result of the world falling in love with this idea(l) of indigenous peoples always being able to adapt and guiding the rest of us on how to live in midst of change, international politics has become rapt in a fantasy of ever-adaptive indigeneity. Indigenous peoples have become the model for the rest of the world to follow in how to live sustainably and to accommodate one's life to changing conditions. This is the political role on the basis of which the peoples are included. Reid and Chandler (2018) go so far as to claim that indigeneity has become an archetype for the subjectivity that neoliberal politics desires. According to this desire, we should all embrace, become aware of and foster our adaptive capacities—in a world where everyone is supposed to secure themselves—and by doing so 'become indigenous'.

It is extremely noteworthy that the obsession of international politics with adaptation and indigeneity not only invokes the concept 'adaptation' itself but appears in more subtle forms and in inscribed assumptions of flexibility and adjustment. The expectation of adaptation manifests itself in the call for indigenous agency, in the need for the peoples to sustain their authenticity and in a politics of compensation. All these are seemingly well-meaning tropes that bear a promise of something better, be it more political leverage, acknowledgment of traditional practices or financial redress. In fact, the tropes are powerful technologies of neoliberal politics that place expectations on indigeneity. The call for agency translates into indigenous peoples being required to empower and govern themselves, to build on their active role by dint of their indigeneity. For the peoples to be recognized and become entitled to certain rights and positions, they must meet a demand placed on them to sustain and reproduce an authenticity and distinctiveness. However, at the same time, the peoples need to adapt to changes in their environments. It is here that the politics of compensation comes into play: the presumption is that indigenous peoples will adapt to changes; added to this is the promise of (potentially) receiving various forms of financial, legal, social or territorial compensation if they do (Lindroth and Sinevaara-Niskanen 2014).

The attempts to address and resolve the unresolved issues relating to the use of lands and natural resources make visible the distorted premises on which negotiations on such issues take place—negotiations that are said to be conducted in 'partnership' with indigenous peoples (Nuttall 2010). The UN guidelines for conducting business that may have an impact on indigenous peoples are a vivid example of how the peoples' supposed role as partners in negotiations has not changed the fundamental power set-up and the primacy of the interests of the global economy. The Guiding Principles on Business and Human Rights that the UN has put forward are based on the idea of 'protect, respect and remedy' (Office of the High Commissioner for Human Rights 2011). According to these guidelines, indigenous peoples and their rights are to be protected and respected by states and, for example, corporations undertaking projects on indigenous territories. In case these measures fail, as in many cases they have, the guidelines advice that indigenous peoples are to be compensated in a way that remedies the loss of and damage to their livelihood and culture. A similar economy-driven approach to the struggle over natural resources prevails within the ambit of the Arctic Council (Sinevaara-Niskanen 2015), an idea that one could calculate monetary value to cultural practices or access to, for example, fresh water. The global economy is represented as a given, a necessity to which indigenous and local economies and peoples must adjust, and by doing so, they might potentially gain some monetary compensation.

Adaptation is presented and celebrated, by international politics and indigenous peoples alike, as something that secures and saves indigenous lives. But what is the indigeneity that is formed through the constant requirement of adaptation? The relationship between the governor and the governed remains intact: it is not Western values and expectations, but rather indigenous cultures and livelihoods that must accommodate themselves to the changing conditions. What is more, no matter how skilled indigenous peoples are in adapting to changes, there are always significant facets of indigenous values, understanding and practices that are removed or excluded from society (see also Brigg 2007). The never-ending adjustments that indigenous peoples must make mean that they remain Others and excluded.

While it may seem that adaptive indigeneity is the saving grace for humankind, in reality what we see at work is the 'indigeneity on-demand' of neoliberal politics whereby subjects cope by themselves and are responsible for their own well-being and existence, no matter the conditions. This adaptive 'indigeneity on-demand' valorizes and evokes certain modes of indigeneity: it is a statement on what the 'proper' indigenous subject is. This is not to say that indigenous peoples are not adaptive or that they should not adapt. However, adaptation as an unquestioned presumption of politics—a politics that is built on colonial grounds—and of a certain kind of indigenous 'being', existence and agency marks the continuation of power relations once declared historical, that is, ones only to be found in history books. The praise for the adaptive capacities of indigenous peoples—tantamount to indigeneity being flexible—is among the essential building blocks of 'proper' indigenous subjectivity in the eyes of international politics.

Pining for Peculiarity

The emphases on indigenous peoples' vulnerability and their adaptive capacity are elements of what can be called "exclusive inclusion" (see also Rifkin 2009; Brigg 2007; Ahmed 2012, on discursive practices of inclusive exclusion). By this, we mean the political moves that valorize certain alleged features of indigeneity while ignoring others (O'Malley 1996; on the similar problematique of oppressive authenticity, see Sissons 2005). As O'Malley (1996, p. 162) has described it, selective valorization means the "neutralization, suppression or eschewal of those aspects which are seen as counterproductive, hostile or incompatible with the project of rule". The inclusion of indigenous peoples in international politics observes this same tactic amounting to partial inclusion.

Collis and Webb (2014), referring to a similar type of problematique, talk about the 'double act' of seeing and not seeing that has historically defined the relations between Natives and Settlers. The politics of forgetting has meant a deliberate erasure of the peoples from society. As Collis and Webb point out, the history of making indigenous peoples invisible has been extreme where their languages, cultures, values and beliefs are concerned. In a similar way, contemporary politics, which seems rife with apologies, inclusion and recognition, still considers indigenous peoples invisible "except insofar as they constitute either a problem, or a decorative feature" (Collis and Webb 2014, p. 494).

One visible and valorized feature in current international politics, as the examples in the contexts of the Arctic Council and the UN Permanent Forum show, is the special relationship that indigenous peoples are perceived to have with the environment (Lindroth and Sinevaara-Niskanen 2014). Here, the embrace of certain alleged qualities of indigeneity is a situation of give-and-take: in making claims of discrimination and narrating vulnerability in the face of environmental degradation—and as "a community defined by some shared features" (Butler 2004, p. 24)—indigenous peoples need to present themselves as a distinct and recognizable group. What is expected from this community or group is a connectedness to the land and the local surroundings, which are—or so it is hoped—local, remote, rural and traditional. Recognition of that position of vulnerability then grants the peoples the status of stakeholders and knowledge providers. The political space of indigeneity is earned by providing evidence of the ability to deliver knowledge and stakeholdership that derive from vulnerability. Once this political position is earned, however, indigenous peoples, rather than being seen as the ones fundamentally changing the course of politics, are expected to perform their expertise in how to adapt to the permanent condition of vulnerability. Thus, gaining a political status on these premises ultimately means that the peoples enter a constrained position, one in which they can raise only certain, very limited concerns. The give-and-take of inclusion that is based on selective valorization and the conscious exclusion of more nuanced and troubling aspects of indigeneity translate into indigenous peoples having little room to argue for new agendas or to exert influence.

Selective valorization relies on and enhances the existing, constructed distinctions between indigenous peoples and other actors in international politics. In the Arctic Council and the Permanent Forum, international environmental politics is filled with dichotomies that reproduce the 'natives' and 'settlers' of global politics. The roles of the actors in international politics are cast in the polar opposites of 'traditional ecological knowledge vs. Western science', 'bearers of environmental risks vs. polluters' and 'peoples living on the land vs. the industrialized world'. This is one of the principal ways in which the peculiar otherness of indigeneity isconstantly reproduced. The inclusion of indigenous peoples has not erased the need and desire to make a distinction between what is considered to be at the core of politics and what and who are at the margins. As Sissons (2005, p. 39) notes, "distinctions between 'native' and 'settler' are continuously reproduced, although always in new guises." What is entailed in the political inclusion of indigenous peoples is the requirement for indigeneity to fulfill the fantasy of distinctive otherness. Indigenous peoples must look, sound and behave indigenous.

Otherness includesthe idea that 'the other' has less power and, accordingly, is in need of protection and special measures. In relation to indigenous peoples, assuming such 'otherness' is a continuation of historical civilizing colonialism, in which indigenous peoples were targets of various practices, measures and regulations in the name of releasing them from their disadvantaged situations. The contemporary special measures to protect the peoples, made in the name of care for the peoples, their practices and cultures, include setting aside a separate 'slot' for indigeneity. In both the UN Permanent Forum and the Arctic Council, a new category of participants has been created in order to accommodate indigenous representatives. In the Arctic Council, this comprises the Permanent Participants, who have equal access and footing with states in the work of the Council. It is noteworthy that the choice was to create separate categories, rather than, for example, imposing quotas that would require states to include indigenous representatives in their delegations. At the moment, it is up to the member states whether they want to strengthen indigenous participation further by including indigenous representatives. In the context of the UN, the Permanent Forum is, in itself, a separate 'slot' for indigeneity. It is one of many advisory bodies in the UN and although it is said to be the focal point for indigenous peoples in the organization, it has not meant structural inclusion of indigenous representative beyond the given slot. Inclusion of indigenous peoples in the UN through the Permanent Forum has not set any binding requirements for states to accommodate indigenous issues on their agendas any more than before or to a greater extent than they are willing to do so.

A separate slot for indigeneity can also be seen in the content and procedures of politics in the UN Permanent Forum and the Arctic Council. For example, in the UN Permanent Forum, traditional prayers of indigenous peoples are an integral part of the annual sessions. Prayers have been included despite the fact that religious practices are not usually allowed in the UN, which aims to be an equally neutral territory for all nations regardless of religion, race or other socio-cultural categories with which one might identify (Lindroth 2011; Dahl 2012, pp. 38–39). In the work of the Arctic Council, which is strongly defined by the production of knowledge concerning the Arctic and its inhabitants, the treatment of the peoples as something 'separate' can be seen in the division of Arctic issues into general and indigenous ones. It is very common that the reports and recommendations produced under the auspices of the Council have separate sections on indigenous concerns (e.g. Arctic Climate Impact Assessment 2005). The integration of indigenous peoples into the work of the Council has not meant that Arctic interests and knowledge have merged; indigenous issues remain separate, 'special' questions.

The process of giving indigenous peoples a separate slot serves to portray international politics as more diverse, inclusive and tolerant. Indigenous peoples make international politics look more attractive and literally more colorful by 'decorating' political institutions with their presence and wearing their traditional costumes. In the UN, for example, there are no clear requirements for the peoples to wear traditional attire, but for the purposes of making politics, appearing 'traditional' and 'indigenous' fulfills the expectation of particularity and can be used as a political tactic. It is a conscious choice on the part of the peoples themselves to utilize (Lindroth 2011). This 'slot' defined by traditionality and otherness ends up locking indigenous peoples and their concerns into their distinctiveness. Gaining the separate slot is success of a kind, but the inability to cross the boundaries of that slot means that indigenous issues can never enter the sphere of 'common issues'. Indigenous concerns, as a result, are not able to enter the platforms that would enable them to challenge, transform or even contribute to what is considered common beyond the specificity of the indigenous category that, for example, the UN Permanent Forum represents. In a similar vein, Cameron (2012, p. 108) notes that in the context of indigenous peoples' participation and discussions on the use of natural resources, the agency accorded to local communities is limited to having a say in the issues relating to livelihoods that are traditionally perceived as local, such as herding and gathering. By contrast, indigenous views are not solicited, for example, on issues pertaining to non-renewable resources despite the fact that these resources have an equally strong presence in the daily life of indigenous communities.

Tellingly, support for indigenous peoples' political agency is considered important in environmental discussions. However, as Sissons (2005, p. 24) points out, when the support is confined to the alleged relationship to nature, it dilutes the significant and specific challenges that indigeneity poses to states. The shift to "more generalized projects of eco- ethnicity and cultural survival", as Sissons asserts, leads to a consideration of indigeneity not in relation to colonization but rather in terms of relative closeness to nature. Accordingly, the idea of 'eco-indigenism' reproduces the polar opposites of Settlers and Natives in global politics. The traditional and environmental slot given to indigenous peoples categorizes indigeneity and indigenous politics as 'primitivist' areas of nature and culture and limits them to these, in contrast to Western rationality, which is destructive of nature (Sissons 2005, pp. 23–24; see also Nadasdy 2005 on indigenous stereotypes and Western environmentalism). The category of 'primitivist' also evokes a call for the adaptive capacities of indigenous peoples.

The expectation of peculiar otherness, while it may enable indigenous peoples' agency, strongly essentializes indigeneity. The allegedly special relationship of the peoples to the environment becomes "defined as one thing: the lone voice of truth, the virtuous defenders of an environment that is being destroyed by the rapaciousness greed for resources" (Rutherford 2007, p. 301). Despite the heterogeneity among indigenous peoples, indigeneity becomes fixed—also by indigenous peoples themselves—as a characteristic that is shared by all indigenous peoples. The political language in which this process is couched, describing the threats and risks facing the collective existence of indigenous peoples, binds indigeneity to community. As environmental actors, indigenous peoples become defined not as individuals but as collectives, as 'peoples'. This is one way of cementing a distinction between indigenous peoples and other political actors. The emphasis on community is visible in the Arctic Human Development Report, considered the leading document on the social developments in the region, the conclusion of which notes:

> More generally, our study has directed attention to a distinction between two fundamentally different perspectives on human development. One approach – we may call it the western approach – starts with the individual and asks how individuals are faring in terms of any number of criteria like life expectancy, education, material well-being, and so forth. An alternative approach – reflected in many indigenous cultures – starts with the community or the social group and views human development through the lens of community viability. Successful individuals are those who make major contributions to the well-being of their communities. (Arctic Human Development Report 2004, p. 241)

The peculiar otherness of indigeneitycan be seen to have two components: indigenous peoples are expected to be the distinguishable other, traditional, local, vulnerable and bound to their environment, and assumed to have a commitment to and an innate need to care for the community. It is this aspect of caring for what you allegedly are, for your surroundings and community that international politics has now also harnessed in the quest for global adaptation. The expectation of adaptive indigeneity makes fulfilling the category of the peculiar other even more demanding. In addition to providing evidence for eco-indigenism, the peoples must not only demonstrate their vulnerability but to demonstrate their abilities to cope and adjust. Indeed, the peculiar otherness that international politics desires keeps slipping from the peoples' grasp. It is a fantasy; it is always unreal, essentialized, romanticized and normative and thus impossible to fulfill. The positioning of indigenous peoples as those in need of fulfilling the fantasy marks the very essence of the power trained on indigeneity.

Smothered by Care

How is one to dissect this newly emerged concern for indigenous peoples and the way of being that they are understood to epitomize? In our view, the inclusion of indigenous peoples and the alleged features of indigeneity, done in the name 'doing good' for the peoples, is a direct continuation of colonial practices designed to either eradicate or civilize them. Fundamentally, inclusion is about erasing certain elements of indigeneity while fostering and enhancing others. In politics, where otherness is the condition for including indigenous peoples, the care 'lavished on' the alleged attributes of indigeneity is, in effect, a violence of sorts. The inclusion and nourishment of the fantasy of indigeneity as different, other and peculiar, stifles the lived realities of the peoples. The elements of contemporary indigeneity, such as urban living, engagement in market-based industries, as well as the diminished role of the local community and the impossibility of adapting to the severe changes in environments, are cast aside. There is little or no room for these considerations in the indigeneity that international politics has created an affective relationship to. As long as it is the essentializing fantasy of indigeneity that international politics pursues, celebrates and officially acknowledges, that politics will fail to recognize any other form of indigeneity and inclusion of indigenous peoples will remain an illusion.

The issues that become recognized politically as causes for concern in relation to indigeneity are the peoples' allegedly close relationship to the environment, their vulnerability in the midst of a changing world and the skills and knowledge they bring to bear in adapting to changes. The attention devoted to these attributes, as noted, gives leverage to the peoples in certain issues, but the kindness offered is conditional. The care for indigeneity that accords it a particular political agency and presence entails conditions to be met: indigeneity rests "on specific relationships between peoples, places and cultures and as distinguishing some peoples as natives relative to others" (Merlan 2009, p. 306). The current 'care' of international politics fosters requirements whereby indigenous peoples must, among other things, maintain cultures that are distinct enough and relationships to the land that are distinguishable enough from the norm.

A similar type of care can be seen in the legal framework that requires indigenous peoples to produce performance and evidence in order to appear before the law in the first place. Within the framework of liberal rights, as Birrell (2016, p. 89) points out, a recognizable indigeneity is required "for the purposes of reclamation of land and waters or the assertion of political and cultural rights." However, in reality, arguing for such rights on the grounds of authenticity, traditionality and continuity—criteria that the law insists on—is in many cases impossible for the peoples. This applies especially to the most marginalized, those whose lives have been pervaded by colonial policies of assimilation, resettlement and the presence of settlers (see also Birrell 2016). For example, ILO Convention No. 169 on the rights of indigenous and tribal peoples, an outcome of negotiations in international politics, sets certain criteria for indigeneity. The Convention has sparked a debate over which groups are entitled to the status of indigenous people (Joona 2010), that is, what the 'qualifications' for that status are. Meeting the criteria for what it means to be indigenous, within the legal framework, can become an endeavor doomed to failure, as providing watertight genealogical evidence of one's past or connectedness to land is based on the current legal and political interpretation of past events. The settling of a previously nomadic indigenous family in a permanent dwelling could be interpreted either as a choice made of the family's own free will or as move compelled by the colonial reality. The law exerts its power by making arbitrary decisions on what type of indigeneity and alterity is deserving of its protection; it reserves to itself the right to define whether the indigenous person who became a farmer any longer fulfills the criteria of authenticity, traditionality and continuity. Law's violent nature is inscribed in its ability to negate the very premises on which the colonized seek justice.

In viewing the recent care for indigenous agency and subjectivity as new camouflage for colonial power, our approach to examining the inclusion of indigenous peoples and indigeneity differs significantly from that applied in earlier scholarship. Previous studies have interpreted the institutional and structural developments in the UN and the Arctic Council, as well as the peoples' improved political position, as progress (Morgan 2011; Axworthy et al. 2012). The concern for the engagement of indigenous peoples in international politics and the well-meaning attention to their allegedly special qualities and features has been viewed as a signal that states and international political arenas are meeting the peoples halfway. Some studies have even argued that a reorganization of power has taken place (Xanthaki 2007; Shadian 2009). The often-heard phrases are that the UN Permanent Forum and the Arctic Council are exemplary institutions that embody the international concern for indigeneity and that are pioneers in making international politics less hierarchical.

In our view, the political and legal care for the 'essence' of indigeneity marks, once again, a forceful intervention into what indigeneity should be and become. If one looks at the past colonial setting, where others set the terms of what indigeneity was assumed to be, to perform and to pursue, there is nothing new in the current set-up. In discussing contemporary colonial power, it becomes not only relevant to recognize the power entailed in the requirement of exceptionality placed on indigeneity but to probe why and how political power reduces indigeneity to otherness. The valorization and embrace of indigenous exceptionality and otherness seem like well-meaning care for vulnerable peoples but signal an exercise of power over indigeneity that is no less limiting and controlling than others. The relations between Native and Settler merely appear to have become more equal and just.

It is the conditions set for 'earning' concern and care that deserve critical attention. As care, at the outset, has been considered something 'good' and something to hope for, the highly essentialized requirements set for indigeneity in return for care have gone unseen, untouched, unproblematized and taken for granted. Indigenous peoples can never achieve full eligibility for care. This means that entering global politics is no more than a struggle to persevere in a limbo designed and ruled by others who see only the indigeneity that they want to see. The benevolent care of international politics marks, in effect, a struggle indigeneity must undertake to exist in the 'right way'.

References

Agrawal, Arun. 2005. *Environmentality. Technologies of Government and the Making of Subjects*. Durham: Duke University Press.

Ahmed, Sara. 2012. *On Being Included: Racism and Diversity in Institutional Life*. Durham: Duke University Press.

Arctic Climate Impact Assessment. 2005. Cambridge: Cambridge University Press.

Arctic Human Development Report. 2004. Akureyri: Stefansson Arctic Institute.

———. 2015. *Regional Processes and Global Linkages*. Copenhagen: Nordisk Ministerråd.

Axworthy, Timothy S., Timo Koivurova, and Waliul Hasanat, eds. 2012. *The Arctic Council: Its Place in the Future of Arctic Governance*. Toronto: Walter & Duncan Gordon Foundation.

Bastidas, Edith. 2008. Presenting the Declaration of the Preparatory Meeting for the 7th session of the UN PF, held 3–4 April 2008 in Santa Cruz de la Sierra, Bolivia. 22 April. Statements are available at the DoCip website. https://www.docip.org/en/indigenous-peoples-at-the-un/permanent-forum. Accessed 4 June 2017.

Birrell, Kathleen. 2016. *Indigeneity: Before and Beyond the Law*. Abingdon: Routledge.

Briceño, Sálvano. 2008. Director. Secretariat of the International Strategy for Disaster Reduction (UN/ISDR). Statement at the 7th Session of the UN Permanent Forum, delivered by Paula Uski, Associate Expert, UN/ISDR New York Liaison Office. 21 April. Statements are available at the DoCip website. https://www.docip.org/en/indigenous-peoples-at-the-un/permanent-forum. Accessed 4 June 2017

Brigg, Morgan. 2007. Biopolitics Meets Terrapolitics: Political Ontologies and Governance in Settler-Colonial Australia. *Australian Journal of Political Science* 42 (3): 403–417.

Butler, Judith. 2004. *Precarious Life. The Powers of Mourning and Violence*. London: Verso.

Cameron, Emilie. 2012. Securing Indigenous Politics: A Critique of the Vulnerability and Adaptation Approach to the Human Dimensions of Climate Change in the Canadian Arctic. *Global Environmental Change* 22 (1): 103–114.

Collis, Paul, and Jen Webb. 2014. The Visible and the Invisible: Legacies of Violence in Contemporary Australian Aboriginal Contexts. *Journal of Australian Studies* 38 (4): 490–503.

Dahl, Jens. 2012. *The Indigenous Space and Marginalized Peoples in the United Nations*. New York: Palgrave Macmillan.

Djonkou, Djankou. 2008. Representative to the UN and Director, International Labour Organization (ILO). Statement at the 7th Session of the UN Permanent Forum. April 21. Statements are available at the DoCip website. https://www.docip.org/en/indigenous-peoples-at-the-un/permanent-forum. Accessed 4 June 2017.

Evans, Brad, and Julian Reid. 2014. *Resilient Life. The Art of Living Dangerously*. Cambridge, Polity.

Fineman, Martha Albertson. 2013. Equality, Autonomy, and the Vulnerable Subject in Law and Politics. In *Vulnerability. Reflections on a New Ethical Foundation for Law and Politics*, ed. Martha Albertson Fineman and Anna Grear, 13–27. Farnham: Ashgate.

Fiu Mataese Elisara. 2008. Executive Director, OLSSI, Samoa. Statement at the 7th Session of the UN Permanent Forum 22 April. Statements are available at the DoCip website. https://www.docip.org/en/indigenous-peoples-at-the-un/permanent-forum. Accessed 4 June 2017.

Furedi, Frank. 2008. Fear and Security: A Vulnerability-led Policy Response. *Social Policy & Administration* 42 (6): 645–661.

Heinämäki, Leena. 2009. Rethinking the Status of Indigenous Peoples in International Environmental Decision-Making: Pondering the Role of Arctic Indigenous Peoples and the Challenge of Climate Change. In *Climate governance in the Arctic*, ed. Koivurova Timo, E. Carina, H. Keskitalo, and Nigel Bankes, 207–262. London: Springer.

Joona, Tanja. 2010. International Norms and Domestic Practices in Regard to ILO Convention, No. 169—With Special Reference to Articles 1 and 13–19. *International Community Law Review* 12 (2): 213–260.

Laub, Regina. 2008. Food and Agriculture Organization. Statement in the 7th Session of the Permanent Forum. Statements are available at the DoCip website. https://www.docip.org/en/indigenous-peoples-at-the-un/permanent-forum. Accessed 4 June 2017.

Li, Tania Murray. 2007. *The Will to Improve: Governmentality, Development, and the Practice of Politics.* Durham: Duke University Press.

Lindroth, Marjo. 2006. Indigenous-State Relations in the UN: Establishing the Indigenous Forum. *Polar Record* 42 (3): 239–248.

———. 2011. Paradoxes of Power: Indigenous Peoples in the Permanent Forum. *Cooperation and Conflict* 46 (4): 542–561.

Lindroth, Marjo, and Heidi Sinevaara-Niskanen. 2014. Adapt or Die? The Biopolitics of Indigeneity—From the Civilising Mission to the Need for Adaptation. *Global Society* 28 (2): 180–194.

Martello, Marybeth Long. 2008. Arctic Indigenous Peoples as Representations and Representatives of Climate Change. *Social Studies of Science* 38 (3): 351–376.

Merlan, Francesca. 2009. Indigeneity. Global and Local. *Current Anthropology* 50 (3): 303–333.

Morgan, Rhiannon. 2011. *Transforming Law and Institution: Indigenous Peoples, the United Nations and Human Rights.* Farnham: Ashgate.

Nadasdy, Paul. 2005. Transcending the Debate over the Ecologically Noble Indian: Indigenous Peoples and Environmentalism. *Ethnohistory* 52 (2): 291–331.

Nuttall, Mark. 2010. *Pipeline Dreams: People, Environment, and the Arctic Energy Frontier.* Copenhagen: IWGIA.

O'Malley, Pat. 1996. Indigenous Governance. *Economy and Society* 25 (3): 310–326.

Office of the High Commissioner for Human Rights. 2011. Guiding Principles for Business and Human Rights: Implementing the United Nations 'Protect, Respect and Remedy' Framework. http://www.ohchr.org/Documents/Publications/GuidingPrinciplesBusinessHR_EN.pdf. Accessed 4 June 2017.

Olsson, Gunilla. 2008. Executive Director. International Fund for Agricultural Development (IFAD). Statement at the 7th Session of the UN Permanent Forum. 21 April. Statements are available at the DoCip website. https://www.docip.org/en/indigenous-peoples-at-the-un/permanent-forum. Accessed 4 June 2017.

Parajuli, Pramod. 2004. Revisiting Gandhi and Zapata: Motion of Global Capital, Geographies of Difference and the Formation of Ecological Ethnicities. In *The Way of Development: Indigenous Peoples, Life Projects and Globalization*, ed. Mario Blaser, Harvey Feit, and Glenn McRae, 235–255. London: Zed Press.

Permanent Forum on Indigenous Issues. 2008. Report on the Seventh Session. April 21–May 2. Economic and Social Council Official Records supplement No. 23. UN: New York. http://undocs.org/E/2008/43(SUPP). Accessed 4 June 2017.

Reid, Julian. 2012. The Disastrous and Politically Debased Subject of Resilience. *Development Dialogue* 58: 67–79.

Reid, Julian, and David Chandler. 2018. Being in Being. *The European Legacy* 23(1).

Rifkin, Mark. 2009. Indigenizing Agamben. Rethinking Sovereignty in Light of the "Peculiar" Status of Native Peoples. *Cultural Critique* 73: 88–124.

Rosay, André B. 2016. *Violence Against American Indian and Alaska Native Women and Men.* National Institute of Justice Research Report. Washington, DC: US Department of Justice. https://www.ncjrs.gov/pdffiles1/nij/249736.pdf. Accessed 2 June 2017.

Rutherford, Stephanie. 2007. Green Governmentality: Insights and Opportunities in the Study of Nature's Rule. *Progress in Human Geography* 31 (3): 291–307.

Sejersen, Frank. 2015. *Rethinking Greenland and the Arctic in the Era of Climate Change. New Northern Horizons.* Abingdon: Routledge.

Shadian, Jessica M. 2009. Revisiting Politics and Science in the Poles: IPY and the Governance of Science in Post-Westphalia. In *Legacies and Change in Polar Science. Historical, Legal and Political Reflections on the International Polar Year*, ed. Jessica M. Shadian and Monica Tennberg, 35–62. Surrey: Ashgate.

Sinevaara-Niskanen, Heidi. 2015. Vocabularies for Human Development: Arctic Politics and the Power of Knowledge. *Polar Record* 51 (2): 191–200.

Sissons, Jeffrey. 2005. *First Peoples. Indigenous Cultures and Their Futures.* London: Reaktion Books.

Smith, Heather A. 2007. Disrupting the Global Discourse on Climate Change: The Case of Indigenous Voices. In *The Social Construction of Climate Change. Power, Knowledge, Norms and Discourses*, ed. Mary E. Petterger, 197–216. Hampshire: Ashgate.

Statistics Canada. 2006. Housing Conditions.. http://www.statcan.gc.ca/pub/89-645-x/2010001/housing-logement-eng.htm. Accessed 2 June 2017.

Sutton, Peter. 2009. *The Politics of Suffering. Indigenous Australia and the End of the Liberal Consensus.* Carlton: Melbourne University Press.

Tauli-Corpus, Victoria. 2008. Chairperson of the Permanent Forum. Statement at the 7th session of the Permanent Forum. Statements are available at the DoCip website. https://www.docip.org/en/indigenous-peoples-at-the-un/permanent-forum. Accessed 4 June 2017.

Tennberg, Monica. 1998. *The Arctic Council. A Study in Governmentality*. Rovaniemi: University of Lapland.
Watson, Irene. 2015. *Aboriginal Peoples, Colonialism and International Law. Raw Law*. Abingdon: Routledge.
Xanthaki, Alexandra. 2007. *Indigenous Rights and United Nations Standards: Self-Determination, Culture and Land*. Cambridge: Cambridge University Press.

CHAPTER 4

The Neoliberal Embrace of Resilient Indigeneity

The Quest for Resilience

The acknowledged relationship of indigenous peoples to the environment, as well as the vulnerability assumed in that relationship and the peoples' capacities to adapt despite the radical changes that they have faced, constructs the exceptional indigeneity that global politics is calling for. That is, as discussed in the previous chapter, this exceptionality is what the peoples are required to perform and reproduce. More importantly, as we will argue in this chapter, the nurturing of peculiar, distinguishable indigeneity draws on the perception of indigeneity as defined through resilience.

Resilience has become a policy buzzword in debates on development in its various forms (e.g. Chandler and Coaffee 2017). The term and the quest for greater capacities on the part of subjects have figured prominently in discussions on environmental and climatic changes and on issues such as well-being, the distribution of global wealth and poverty reduction. Resilience has become increasingly central, particularly where discussions center on the management of uncertainty and risks, and 'building resilience' is presented as an answer to the unpredictability of the future (Walker and Cooper 2011; Welsh 2014). Indeed, as Welsh notes (2014, p. 21), "[r]esilience holds out the promise of knowing 'when' change enters a system, in turn holding out the promise of managing change, of ameliorating its unacceptable effects".

M. Lindroth, H. Sinevaara-Niskanen, *Global Politics and Its Violent Care for Indigeneity*,
https://doi.org/10.1007/978-3-319-60982-9_4

As far back as 2004, the Arctic Human Development Report noted that "the resistance and resilience of Arctic cultures and societies are as impressive as the changes they have so far managed to successfully negotiate" (Arctic Human Development Report 2004, p. 45). In a similar vein, the World Economic and Social Survey, published in 2016 by the Department of Economic and Social Affairs of the United Nations Secretariat and titled *Climate Change Resilience: An Opportunity for Reducing Inequalities*, highlights local knowledge as a crucial element in building climate resilience:

> Because the most intense and direct effects of climate events are experienced at the local level, scoping (or identifying) objectives and risks can benefit tremendously from the knowledge accumulated by local communities. There is an obvious role for this knowledge in tailoring interventions to the local context and conditions; for example, local knowledge can inform technical assessments of adaptation options while those assessments can inform local communities on how to better deal with climate change... Tapping into local knowledge has brought significant benefits in terms of climate resilience [...] (World Economic and Social Survey 2016, p. 89)

The discussion on resilience has carved out a special position for indigenous peoples. For example, the UN survey on Climate Change Resilience and the Arctic Resilience Report, both published in 2016, direct particular attention to indigenous peoples when discussing causes of vulnerability, abilities to adapt and potential risks of maladaptation, which are seen, respectively, as necessitating, supporting or threatening the resilience of communities. Indeed, 'resilience' increasingly defines current discussions on indigenous peoples. The political parlance designates the peoples as vulnerable and being at risk but, at the same time, as capable of adapting and surviving. The idea(l) of indigenous peoples as being resilient also prevails in social scientific and ecological research on global changes (e.g. Forbes 2013; Hovelsrud and Smit 2010). The studies have largely focused on local events and have viewed resilience as a solution to the various challenges and situations that indigenous peoples face. Resilience has been considered a collective and cultural strength that indigenous peoples can harness in addressing challenges.

It is the resilience of indigenous peoples that enables them to cope with impending changes and to prosper. In the midst of climatic changes and increased extraction of natural resources, for example, indigenous peoples are portrayed as 'persistent local communities' and as communities that 'constantly adapt' and whose 'resilience is to be supported'. By dint of the peoples' indigeneity—its alleged strengths, such as a close relationship to the environment and traditional knowledge—they are perceived as exceptionally well equipped to cope and persist. Their persistence is also manifest in their attempts to revive their own cultural, political and legal practices (Corntassel 2012).

The concept of resilience, as well as the concepts of vulnerability and adaptation discussed in Chap. 3, originates in the natural sciences. The original aim of studying the processes of ecosystems recovering, rebounding and resuming their original state after being exposed to a stressor has morphed into an interest in the social and its ability to behave accordingly (Walker and Cooper 2011; Welsh 2014). In its original usage, the concept was not a policy term but a tool for understanding environmental stressors, ecological cycles caused by pollution and the capacities of the environment to accommodate and renew itself in the case of extreme change. The trickling down of resilience and application of the concept in the fields of 'the social' and 'the human' is in line with the interests of global politics in mapping and managing the social world and its agents (e.g. Neumann and Sending 2010; Joseph 2012). The emergence of resilience as a social attribute has shifted the political attention to the subjects, practices, abilities and injuries of the social world.

The Arctic provides an example of the ways in which concepts of science mesh with the aims, practices and aspirations of politics to an extent where terms become policy buzzwords. The region and its politics have been described as "an international scientific laboratory", an area "framed by science" (Tennberg 2009, p. 191). This intertwining of science and policy can be seen in sharp relief in the working groups of the Arctic Council, doubtless a consequence of the Council's strong commitment to the environmental sciences from the very beginning. The working groups have different thematic focuses that reflect different research interests. For example, the working group on Conservation of Arctic Flora and Fauna concentrates on issues of environmental protection, whereas the expertise of the Sustainable Development Working Group encompasses questions of social sustainability. The work of the Council is carried on mainly in the projects of the working groups and the resulting popularized science reports, of which the Arctic Resilience Report is a striking example. These reports are published under the auspices of the Council and its working groups and form the basis of the future actions of the Council. In the course of this work, a significant number of scientific terms have been adopted for use in politics—resilience being one—and research has received its funding and assignments from politics. Research expertise has, in turn, had a significant role in guiding politics (Sinevaara-Niskanen 2015).

All of this together—the research interest in resilience as a social capacity, the entanglement of research and politics in addressing anticipated global challenges and the heightened interest in the knowledge and abilities of individuals and communities—has meant that resilience has become a ubiquitous concern, an objective to be pursued and a capacity to be built up and nurtured. As an ability to recover and persist despite the impact of external threats, resilience has been made an object of various ways of 'measuring', calculating and even statistical modeling. The concern for individuals' and communities' capacities to cope has also meant mapping their inabilities to do so. Where the abilities to cope and rebound are lacking, the politics and research on resilience talk about maladaptation (e.g. Arctic Resilience Report 2016). The 'erosion' of socio-economic adaptability is considered a threat to communities that have become "unable to change in the face of shocks" (Walker and Cooper 2011, p. 156). For indigenous peoples, the newly found interest in resilience has meant a heightened interest in their struggles, in particular grappling with dramatic changes in their living environments, as well as the discovery of the value of traditional indigenous knowledge, observations and sustainable ways of life. What indigeneity (allegedly) has to offer is local and experience-based knowledge that can inform communities at large in strengthening their resilience in the face of climate change.

Indigenizing Resilience

The assumption of indigenous resilience has become an integral part of the distinctiveness and traditionality that define indigeneity in various political, legal and cultural sites. Resilience, in flesh and blood, has been and continues to be the prime condition of existence for indigenous peoples. If indigenous peoples' resilience has historically meant struggling to stay alive and exist, in the contemporary world, indigenous peoples need to struggle to stay resilient. This means also accommodating themselves to political and legal frameworks by constantly offering evidence that validates their existence and causes. As a result, resilience and indigeneity have become inseparable. Resilience is the celebrated core of what indigeneity is perceived to be, a supposedly innate quality that validates their political and global existence.

The very same elements that make up indigeneity as political subjectivity—their relationship to the environment, as well as vulnerability and adaptation—are the ones that are seen as evidence of their resilience and as constructing a particular way of being that is considered resilient indigeneity. These strands are interlinked and inseparable, but identifiable as elements that contribute to the political and more general assumption that indigenous peoples are particularly adept at accommodating changing conditions and to the world's desire that the peoples do so. A re-reading of these three elements in light of the critical discussion on resilience reveals the tight grip that neoliberal politics has over indigeneity today. It is in the name of these particular and exceptional capacities that indigenous peoples are called upon, included and valued in international politics. This is the common ground of how indigeneity is perceived in international politics, and it is clearly visible in the work of both the Permanent Forum and the Arctic Council.

Care-Taking Indigeneity It is in the face of environmental degradation that care-taking indigeneity is invoked. The political parlance is filled with notions that describe the particular relationship of indigenous peoples to their environments. 'Care for future generations', 'sustainable lifestyles', 'harmony with nature', preserving the environment 'in balance' and a 'stewardship duty' are all often repeated descriptions and features that are understood be a part of indigeneity. On the basis of these features, indigenous peoples are in a position to educate the rest of the world on how to live with respect for the environment. As was stated in the 2008 annual session of the UN Permanent Forum, the peoples can "certainly guide us to making informed decisions on mitigation and adaptation" and that it is "of importance to not only view the indigenous and local communities as victims but more so as valuable agents of change" (MacDonald 2008). Similarly, it has been noted in the Arctic Climate Impact Assessment that indigeneity should be valued because "indigenous observations and perspectives offer great insights" (Arctic Climate Impact Assessment 2005, p. 62). Care and compassion, as well as the ability to impart to others an intimate capacity to care, are among the valorized attributes of indigeneity. For example, traditional indigenous knowledge lacked recognition for a long time, especially in the case of traditional ecological knowledge, but now it seems that it is praised as an alternative 'solution' to the ecological crisis. As the Arctic Resilience Report (2016, p. xvi) notes, "[l]iving in one of the world's most variable biomes means that people of the Arctic, and in particular the Indigenous Peoples of the Arctic, know a great deal about resilience."

There is no doubt regarding the genuine care and worry that indigenous peoples have for their living environments, nor is there reason to question their past or current abilities to cope with changes. However, viewed in critical perspective, perceiving and portraying indigenous peoples as care-takers, and assigning to and requiring of them such a role, is one of the ways in which contemporary global politics calls for resilient indigeneity. The peoples' special relationship to nature and their environmental knowledge bind their destiny to resilience. The logic that obtains here places the peoples in and close to nature and thus assumes that they are able to observe it and adjust their way of life accordingly. The image of indigenous peoples as care-takers relies on very essentialist notions of indigeneity. The assumption of care-taking indigeneity affirms an understanding of indigeneity as inherently traditional. Indigenous peoples are assumed to be living in non-urban settings, to engage in certain nature-based livelihoods and to possess knowledge that is handed down through the generations. For many, this is not the reality, however. They have resettled, willingly or by force, or the continuity of generations has been broken due to the loss of language, imposition of non-indigenous education (e.g. boarding schools) or other negative developments.

Vulnerable Peoples Under Threat Another common way of presenting indigeneity in global politics is a discourse of risk and threat. The role assigned to the peoples is that of (local) vulnerable populations, despite their living environments often having an abundance of natural resources. As the Indigenous Caucus at the 2002 annual session of the UN Permanent Forum stated:

> It is always said that indigenous peoples are among the poorest of the poor and that they belong to the most vulnerable sectors of society. And yet it is also known that the indigenous peoples live in territories that are very rich with natural resources. (Indigenous Caucus 2002)

In the case of climate change, indigenous peoples are represented as "most affected" (Olsson 2008). Their survival is "at risk" and their lives are considered "particularly and immediately" threatened (Bastidas 2008). As UN rhetoric illustrates, it is very common to talk about indigenous peoples as "the poorest and most marginalized groups in the world" (Magga 2002). The position of vulnerable populations is also appropriated by indigenous peoples themselves. The concern for the 'weaker position' of indigenous peoples has caused them to be viewed as a target group which the global community needs to support with special measures. In effect, the emphasis on the vulnerability of indigenous peoples objectifies them; they become the objects of protective actions, which, while perhaps well-intentioned, are nevertheless not designed or implemented by the peoples.

The vulnerability discourse is integral to resilience; vulnerability is a presupposed state. As critical scholars have noted, in the world of insecurity, vulnerability is a "defining condition of existence" and the making of helpless victims at the mercy of their surroundings is "strategically embraced" (Furedi 2008, p. 652, 658; Evans and Reid 2014, p. 21). Politically, vulnerability is used not to solve or eliminate risks but to enhance and exploit a subjectivity that is hierarchically in a lower position:

> To be at risk assigns to the person a passive and dependent role. To be at risk is no longer about what you do – it is about who you are. It is an acknowledgement of powerlessness – at least in relation to that risk. Increasingly, someone defined as being at risk is seen to exist in a permanent condition of vulnerability. (Furedi 2008, p. 656; see also Drichel 2013)

In our view, the Arctic Council and the UN Permanent Forum have been built in response to such vulnerability. For example, the 2016 Arctic Resilience Report continues to perceive the Arctic Council as an asset and a resource for reducing marginalization, poverty and exclusion by building "social capital" (Arctic Resilience Report 2016, p. xv). Tellingly, years after the establishment of these two forums and the inclusion of indigenous peoples in their work, the discussion of indigenous peoples and vulnerability continues to revolve around 'building capacities' (e.g. UNESCO 2012). The statements of the Permanent Forum point out, for example, that there is a need to "empower indigenous peoples to manage their lands in sustainable ways" (Olsson 2008) and "strengthen the abilities of indigenous peoples to negotiate to improve the situations of their peoples" (Reidy 2008). The Arctic Climate Impact Assessment also includes understandings to the effect that indigenous peoples need to apply for funding and to establish an "environmental program with a focus on community planning and increasing understanding about the long-term impacts of climate change" (Arctic Climate Impact Assessment 2005, p. 77). Viewed critically, their vulnerability notwithstanding, the peoples' environmental skills and knowledge are used to promote 'the right kind' of action (O'Malley 1996, p. 201). Although indigenous peoples are perceived to be the care-takers with traditional knowledge, they are still required to educate, empower and improve themselves.

The call for resilience, for which vulnerability is a prime precondition, has fundamentally transformed the way in which international politics deals with the future horizon of risks and threats. It is true that many risks are such that they cannot be avoided, reversed or even predicted, especially in the case of climate change. Yet, this is not to say that the conditions that make indigenous peoples vulnerable could not be ameliorated substantially. With genuine political and legal will, many of the contentious issues between indigenous peoples, states and the relevant societies at large could be resolved by a more just distribution of resources, rights and wealth. For example, the peoples' right to use the land and to benefit from it, discrimination and racism against them and their (lack of) opportunity to decide on the development of their own culture (e.g. Collis and Webb 2014; Sejersen 2015; Austin-Broos and Merlan 2017) still loom large on the agenda. It is most evident that eradicating the vulnerability of indigenous peoples is not even an aim in this era of resilience.

On the contrary, for international politics to recognize indigeneity in the first place, indigeneity must strive to fulfill the requirement of vulnerability, which is based on its being injured. The eradication of indigenous peoples' less privileged position would mean that global politics would lose its ability to draw on the peoples' persistent existence, despite their vulnerability, as a particular example of resilience. In maintaining vulnerability as the precondition of indigenous resilience, politics is not concerned with the specific issues that have caused the indigenous subject's injuries. When vulnerability is understood as a quality of an individual or collective subject, it ceases to be about "specific interactions" and becomes "an abstract lack" within the vulnerable subject (Schott 2013, p. 213). In the case of indigenous peoples, vulnerability appears detached from the unresolved colonial relations and the states' role in producing the peoples' vulnerability. The focus on the vulnerability of indigenous peoples, rather than signaling an effort to overcome the injury and the weaker position of the peoples, entangles vulnerability and resilience, making vulnerability an innate feature, one inseparable from indigeneity.

The Adaptive Indigenous Adaptation is a key element, linked to care and vulnerability, that defines indigenous peoples in international politics. Indigenous peoples at large are seen through the prism of adaptation. Adaptation is portrayed as something that secures and saves indigenous lives as much as it saves others. In the 2008 annual session of the UN Permanent Forum on, statements were delivered highlighting that indigenous peoples "with their traditional knowledge, learned how to cope with changing conditions" (MacDonald 2008) and have the 'skills' to adapt (Caron 2008). The Arctic Resilience Report (2016) also notes that indigenous peoples' skills in coping are very much in demand in light of the dramatic changes anticipated in the future. The peoples and ecosystems in the region are expected to "adapt and even transform themselves as needed" (Arctic Resilience Report 2016, p. xii).

As Joseph (2013, p. 43) argues, knowing how to adapt is a way to survive in the neoliberal world of insecurity. An ability to adapt, to have a heightened awareness of one's surroundings, is an integral element of being resilient. Paradoxically, for indigenous peoples, the ability to adapt and be resilient in the past and the present has meant that the requirement of adaptation imposed on them is never-ending. The continuous existence of indigenous peoples is proof of their past abilities to adapt, and the contemporary global need for adaptation draws on their alleged flexibility and malleability. While the ability to adapt to varying conditions may help one to survive, there is an inscribed assumption that one must constantly build up that ability. Indigenous peoples, given the historical evidence of their possessing special abilities to adapt, are positioned in a category of their own, one resting on the assumption that they will be capable of adapting forever. The juxtaposition of, on the one hand, the peoples' close relationship to nature and vulnerability and, on the other hand, their ability to 'bounce back' has led to their adaptability—and the responsibility for remaining adaptable—becoming a defining element of their existence. Indigenous peoples' (allegedly) intimate connection to environment translates into an expectation that they are to define themselves in relation to their surroundings and the risks and threats facing them there and to adapt to these conditions on their own. At the core of adaptation is devolution of responsibility for the risks associated with the environment to those with local knowledge (e.g. Agrawal 2005; Rutherford 2007), indigenous peoples being one such group. Since indigenous peoples allegedly have a special knowledge of their environment, it is expected that they will be the first to detect environmental changes and will then adapt accordingly.

The requirement that indigenous peoples adapt is hardly confined to discussions on the environment. As a defining element of indigeneity, the need to adapt haunts the peoples in other spheres as well. This expectation of adaptation underpins much of the present emphasis on 'partnership' and 'active agency', which figure among the guiding principles in including indigenous peoples in global politics. For example, the science-policy rhetoric of the Arctic Council describes participation by the indigenous peoples as a form of 'co-management'. The Council has proffered indigenous engagement as "institutional experimentation" and a "meaningful participation" in governing development (Arctic Human Development report 2004, p. 237). In the UN Permanent Forum, the indigenous peoples have a legitimate and established position, yet find themselves between a rock and a hard place. While they may articulate their own agendas, they must conform to political structures and cultures defined by others; clearly they would be ill-advised to exclude themselves from the forums in which their concerns are addressed. Statements made in the UN Permanent Forum sum up their contribution: the "involvement. . .of indigenous peoples is indispensable" (MacDonald 2008) and their "increasing participation" (Caron 2008) is of extreme importance. The institutional requirement to adapt means that the peoples cannot afford to not participate in these forums; otherwise there would be no one to voice and draw attention to their concerns.

Whether the issue is adaptation to institutional practices or to environmental changes, the world does not seem to provide indigenous peoples any alternative courses of action. The peoples need to accommodate themselves to political agendas and processes (e.g. priorities, requirements of consensus, separate 'slots' where actual power is constrained), to changing living conditions (e.g. relocations due to environmental degradation, natural resource extraction or transformation or disappearance of livelihoods) and to cultural expectations set by the legal framework (e.g. distinguishable traditional cultures and practices, proven connections to land). The need for indigeneity to accommodate itself is ever-present and, in many cases, imposed by others as the following excerpt from the Arctic Resilience Report illustrates:

> The resilience of Arctic communities and ecosystems *depends* not only *on* the *commitment* and *imagination* of Arctic people, but also on the active support

> of Arctic countries' governments and other partners. Most of all, the people of the Arctic need support to organize, define challenges in their own terms, and *find their own solutions, knowing that they will have the flexibility* and external backing to implement their plans. (Arctic Resilience Report 2016, p. xvi, emphasis added)

Significantly, for indigenous peoples, adaptation is tantamount to being continuously flexible when being and positioning oneself in the world. And, as the Arctic Resilience Report states, there is no alternative other than finding one's own solutions. Only those who can do so can hope to be deemed worthy of potential support. Whether one regards the historical or contemporary power setting, it becomes apparent that the indigenous peoples have not been the ones who have set the terms or pace of their adaptation; they have been told—as they still are—to just adapt.

The trick with adaptation is that no matter how skillfully indigenous peoples adapt, a significant range of indigenous values, behaviors and practices are still dismissed or excluded. Indigenous peoples must constantly adjust themselves as they continue to be Others and excluded (see also Brigg 2007 and Thisted 2013). The inclusion of indigenous peoples in global politics has not erased them from the rolls of those who need to accommodate themselves to political, legal and social structures designed and set by others. Indeed, as they are constantly called upon to respond to change and adjust to varying situations, the peoples have no choice but to maintain, build and foster their adaptive capacities.

At the Mercy of Its Conditions

The current political set-up that embraces the (alleged) indigenous qualities of care, vulnerability and adaptation is a neoliberal trope. In an era of uncertainty, risks and insecurity—the world as narrated by neoliberalism—the position allocated to indigeneity is that of a subjectivity that will constantly react and accommodate itself to existing or forthcoming events. In the pervasive terms of resilience, the kind of being called for is one who is "endlessly extendable, fit and adaptable" (Dillon 2005, p. 42). This is the type of subjectivity that the world of uncertainty needs from all of us. As Evans and Reid (2014, p. 68) observe, in a neoliberal reality, subjects are to accept "an understanding of life as a permanent process or continual adaptation to threats and dangers which appear outside its control." However, in the case of indigenous peoples, a neoliberal politics that exploits the features considered to form their very essence as resilient marks an even more fundamental—and ultimately colonial—exercise of power. This is a power that, despite being dressed up in well-meaning guises, is a controlling and subjugating form of governing.

If equal distribution of rights was once, at least rhetorically, the primary international political aim prompting inclusion of indigenous peoples, the principal goal today is to enhance the peoples' capacities to adapt, to build up resilience and be self-sufficient. The commitment to adaptability and resourcefulness as parameters for development marks a significant shift in viewing the world and the rights of different subjects in it. As Walker and Cooper (2011, p. 155) aptly observe:

> development for post-colonial poor now consists not in achieving First World standards of urban affluence but in surviving – preferably on the land instead of slums – the after-effects of industrial modernization ... (Walker and Cooper 2011, p. 155)

In this light, the celebration of adaptation as a core feature of indigenous resilience foretells a future where indigenous peoples can exist, be recognized and even valued as subjects of certain kind but may never gain equal rights or wealth. The resilience of indigenous peoples might enable them to persevere in the future, as they have in the past, but it will not make it possible for them to challenge or change the conditions of inequality embedded in this setting.

Originating in studies in systems ecology, the notion of resilience has not been thought of as having political purchase per se. The trickling down and application of the concept to the social world and social phenomena have introduced the ecosystems idea of constantly 'recovering' and 'resuming' into the realm of human subjects and their (in)abilities to do the same. Resilience is called for in subjects both at the individual and collective levels. The resilient subjects who will thrive are those that have the individual capacities to adjust and who commit themselves to the good of their communities. 'Rebounding' after exposure to an unexpected and uncontrolled event might require adjustments in the subject itself, because returning to the 'original state' is often impossible. For example, the resilience of an Arctic community might save its members in the case of extreme flooding, but the resulting changes in fish stocks in the affected river could permanently change the community's diet. In addition, should fishing no longer be a viable livelihood, the residents might be compelled to find new ways of supporting themselves. Resilience could thus afford a community better possibilities to remain in the area that its residents consider home, but often only with substantial sacrifices (Sinevaara-Niskanen and Tennberg 2012).

Whereas the ecological idea of resilience could imply some level of 'rebounding' in the context of the social world, the assumption that a subject 'bounces back' after a trauma, for example, actually denies that the subject's past has any claim to the present. The expectation of the subject's resilience overlooks the wounds of the past. Despite its injury, the subject is assumed to 'get over it' and 'move on'. The call for resilience not only ignores the subject's injuries but also fails to take into account the depth and degree of pain entailed in them. For example, the colonial trauma of the indigenous peoples—centuries-long marginalization and physical abuse, to cite a few—is being lumped together with the other injuries of all those whom the neoliberal political rhetoric is now urging to just 'get over it'. For indigenous peoples, the violence entailed in this current setting of 'resilience' lies precisely in its denying that the wounds of the colonial past might be felt in, and thus have a bearing on, the indigenous present. Suggesting that indigenous subjects should just forget or march on—as resilient subjects do—as if the injury never happened or no longer mattered is colonial brutality in the present.

Indeed, the call for the resilient subject is, as other critical scholars (e.g. Joseph 2013; Evans and Reid 2014; Chandler and Reid 2016) have noted, an exercise of neoliberal power. As Welsh (2014, p. 16) poignantly observes, the call for resilience facilitates

> [...] archetypal governmental technologies of neoliberalism; government at a distance, technologies of responsibilisation, and practices of subjectification that produce suitably prudent autonomous and entrepreneurial subjects in a world of naturalised uncertainty and crisis.

In the neoliberal era, uncertainty is not a given condition or event that one reacts to but a constructed constant condition that justifies certain interventions. The insistence on resilience turns our concern with the world to our own subjectivity (Joseph 2013; Welsh 2014). We are to be concerned for our inner resources in order to cope in and with the world, not to entertain visions that we may change the world that frames our existence.

Today, the features that a proper and responsible indigenous subject is perceived to have—care for the environment, vulnerability and adaptability—are embodiments of resilience. The subjectivity attached to indigeneity is one that copes and is inclined to accommodate itself. This follows the neoliberal script of resilience, which draws on the (allegedly) innate features of subjects and their ability to nurture their adaptive capacities. Building resilience is a matter of governing oneself in a proper way (Furedi 2008; Joseph 2013; Evans and Reid 2014; Welsh 2014). The ways in which indigeneity has become circumscribed by resilience have not only ignored the injury to indigenous peoples but made them responsible for dealing with their circumstances as best they can. In contrast to the colonial past, where indigenous peoples were seen as dependent populations, in the current era of resilience, the peoples are considered 'autonomous' and 'responsible'. In order for the peoples to be autonomous, govern themselves appropriately and manage the risks that they face in a responsible manner, they must assess their own risks, accumulate their knowledge and make 'wise' decisions (Lindroth and Sinevaara-Niskanen 2013, 2014).

International politics, by accommodating indigenous peoples as caretakers, responsibilizes indigenous communities, requiring them to observe, report and be aware of their surrounding conditions. The integration of indigenous knowledge into climate scenarios and modeling and the emphasis on that knowledge is an example of the transfer of responsibility. Encouraging indigenous peoples to observe the changes in their local environments—in the name of care for the peoples and an interest in their supposed special capacities—is a way to bring about the responsible, self-governing and prepared subject that neoliberal politics desires. The neoliberal embrace of care-taking indigeneity means that indigenous peoples must successfully address environmental degradation or other threatening changes that are the after-effects of a world order that has remained, to a large extent, inaccessible to them. Again, the care-taking role leaves the peoples at the mercy of their conditions. As Evans and Reid (2014, p. 9) have also noted, the contemporary neoliberal quest for resilience incorporates a skewed logic for distributing responsibility. The imaginaries of climate catastrophes "author new forms of planetary stewardship which, ironically, tend to apply to native populations in resource-rich areas who have contributed the least to environmental degradation" (Evans and Reid 2014, p. 9).

Indeed, the resilient indigenous peoples are expected to retain their vulnerability—the very attribute that validates their knowledge in adapting—in the face of environmental threats and to bear the responsibility for saving the planet using that very knowledge (Lindroth and Sinevaara-Niskanen 2013). The seemingly well-meaning political care has as its stated aim the emancipation of indigenous peoples, yet it expects indigeneity to be reproduced as an object in need of care. In light of the role of care-taker assigned to indigenous peoples, the particularity of indigenous resilience lies in the peoples being deemed 'vulnerable' as communities. As the excerpt from the Arctic Human Development Report (2004, p. 241) cited above indicates, indigenous worldviews are considered to start "with the community" and "successful individuals are those who make major contributions to the well-being of their communities."

Significantly, the responsibility embedded in indigenous resilience and the construction of the resilient indigenous subject applies not only on the individual but, more importantly, the collective level. Indigeneity is targeted as a feature of a group and subjects who strive to be resilient and have to do so because and on behalf of the whole community. The trickling down to indigenous peoples of environmental responsibility for observing, knowing and, in the end, adapting is a visible sign of a change in who is considered to be the appropriate bearer of responsibility (e.g. Rutherford 2007; Summerville et al. 2008). The threats and risks facing the collective existence of indigenous peoples bind indigeneity and indigenous resilience to the community. One sees a distinction vis-à-vis what is considered an individual-oriented Western world: indigenous peoples are responsibilized as communities. The dichotomy is invoked, yet again, to echo that between the Natives and Settlers. In the resilience frame, reproducing this distinction is a technique of power. The subjects of the Western world are not expected to build their adaptive capacities collectively, for example, in the form of neighborhood groups, extended families or groups with shared interests. Resilient indigeneity, however, is very much a matter of commitment to the community, caring for it, sharing its vulnerabilities and struggling for its survival. The constant political concern for indigenous communities and their vulnerabilities affirms the perceived 'core values' and attributes of indigeneity and the ways in which the expectation of resilience is imposed on it. This coupling of vulnerability and community has given rise to a particular rationality of governing through resilience.

As Evans and Reid (2014, p. 47) have noted, resilience "segregates life on account of its vulnerable qualities." This means that the expectation of resilience is imposed specifically on those who are perceived to be the most vulnerable and with reference to the very features forming that vulnerability.

More significantly, resilience makes distinctions in its treatment of the vulnerable by attuning its expectations to the characteristics of different groups. The power of resilience in governing subjects stems precisely from its not being a universal condition and the requirements it imposes on the vulnerable not being universal either. For indigenous peoples, long excluded from society at large, the role of the community has no doubt been vital. In remote areas, the support, networks and care provided by the community continue to be a lifeline. A range of developments and trends have prompted a concrete concern among the peoples over the future viability of their communities: environmental, political and social changes that have taken place due to climate change, decisions to extract natural resources, cuts in public funding for services in remote areas and declining employment and educational opportunities. The calls for resilient communities, made as they are on the basis of risks and threats facing the communities, are attempts to harness the peoples' concern for their communities to increase the pressure on them to continuously modify themselves. Here, the 'hooks' that resilience seizes, as preconditions and tools for administering indigeneity, are the already wounded parts of indigenous lives, that is, the community, its past injury and future survival. The urge to develop resilient indigenous communities hits a nerve, as it plays on imaginaries of threat to the very things that the peoples are already deeply concerned about and struggling to preserve. Again, the call for resilience treats indigeneity very violently.

The message propagated to subjects in urging resilience is that in order to be saved, one needs to build up one's resourcefulness and responsiveness and that this has to be done despite one's vulnerability. Clearly there is a contradiction in terms here: in the end there is no salvation because no matter how skillful their adaptation and adjustment, subjects remain at the mercy of their conditions, always vigilant and on alert. To be honest, has anything really changed from colonial times if the indigenous subjectivity called for has become a neoliberal subjectivity, which, according to Reid (2012, p. 74, emphasis added), is "capable of making those adjustments **to itself** which enable it to survive"?

What the joyful inclusion of indigenous peoples to international politics has offered to indigenous peoples is precisely the position of a subject that is constantly on call. Both the political rhetoric and institutional maneuvers emphasizing the peoples' abilities and responsibilities to provide 'vital information' contribute to the 'care for future generations' and to provide knowledge and experiences on 'how to adapt' assign them a permanent position of preparedness. It might seem that the inclusion of indigenous peoples and the celebration of their special skills and knowledge, skills that the rest of us have lost, would mean a genuine acknowledgment of what the peoples can contribute. However, when viewed critically, this reaching out to the peoples is nothing more than a transformation on the way in which indigeneity is governed.

Diluting the Political

It has been very common, in politics, public parlance and research alike, to view indigenous peoples' resilience as an asset that has enabled them to survive through the environmental and colonial harshness of the past. The concept has been embraced as an attribute of the peoples without reflecting on its use, consequences and purpose. Resilience has been seen as politically neutral, as Welsh (2014, p. 21) aptly describes:

> [...] sitting comfortably with a consensus rhetoric of criticality (certain practice are 'bad' or unsustainable) yet proffering technocratic solutions (of adaptive management) framed within and using the same (capitalist) logic and vocabulary (of capital and services etc.) that those problems result from.

This assumed neutrality has diverted attention from critically asking what is at stake when indigeneity is defined by, and discussed solely in terms of, adaptation, endurance and persistence.

The recurring representation of indigeneity as adaptive, responsive and flexible, despite the wounds of the colonial past or the given conditions, erodes the political in it. Resilience becomes coupled with indigeneity—as a body of histories, traditions, expectations and self-identifications that are used and (re)claimed politically—and imposes certain (violent) terms on it. First, the never-ending requirement for adaptation, which takes place on terms set by others, places indigeneity in a constant mode of endurance and survival. Ultimately, the adaptation demanded of indigenous peoples might result in death. This meaning that a part of a culture, traditional habit or, in the end, an entire culture ceases to exist. Second, as discussed above, the ideal of the resilient indigenous subject sustains a particular kind of indigeneity, one that fits expectations of its being vulnerable, adaptive and caring. The resilient indigenous subject must be able and willing to fulfill these expectations and to modify and make adjustments to itself according to the given conditions at any given time (Lindroth and Sinevaara-Niskanen 2014, 2016). Third, as a result, the idea(l) of a resilient indigenous people constructs the people as drifting subjects, not as agents of change (on the workings of resilience in general, see also Evans and Reid 2014; Joseph 2013). The reduction of indigeneity to the category of 'the resilient' by overlooking the claims, aspirations and demands of the peoples dilutes the political in indigeneity. As long as indigenous peoples are treated as resilient and no more, neoliberal politics does not have to consider them political. If resilient subjectivity only allows a type of being that must fit in, adapt and extend (see also Duffield 2011a; Reid 2012), it is a positioning meaning that indigeneity cannot harness its political potential and pose a fundamental challenge to the existing order. Originally, of course, this was the principal aim of indigenous movements and organizations, and the inclusion of the peoples in global politics was seen as securing their opportunities to achieve that goal.

By insisting that the peoples have to be resilient, neoliberal politics denies that the wounds of the past put any real claims on the present (Schott 2013). In doing so, the politics refuses to address the surroundings and circumstances that have caused the wounds, the conditions that exist to this day. Instead, it asks, invites and ultimately demands that the indigenous subject has to accommodate itself to the existing conditions, no matter how life-threatening they may be. In its struggle to exist in what is an insecure world, resilient indigeneity must overcome its injuries and wounds. The trauma of indigeneity is not considered to be of a political kind at all, but rather is matter of and for the subject. The focus of resilience on the indigenous subject, instead of its surroundings, is the presence of colonialism today.

The focus on subjects instead of conditions, past or present, transforms the experienced trauma into an issue that the subject must address. As Coulthard (2014, p. 126) insightfully notes, the "bitter indignation and persistent anger at being treated unjustly by a colonial state both historically and in the present..." becomes pathologized as a subjective experience to be healed by the subject or its community. This pathologization signifies the inability of colonial states to comprehend peoples' anger and resentment as consequences of their politics. In this vein, Butler and Athanasiou (2013, p. 87) observe how the status quo is maintained by inscribing injury in the identity of the dispossessed instead of seeking to determine who is responsible for their oppression. All in all, the keenness of politics and the society to treat anger and resentment as an inability of indigenous peoples to 'move on' is a conscious act that strips indigenous politics of the power that could be fueled by these very manifestations of injustice. Where the world pins injury onto the indigenous identity, as a matter to be dealt with solely by the peoples, the injury "cannot be recast as an oppression to be overcome" (Butler and Athanasiou 2013, p. 87). On the contrary, pinningwoundednessonto the indigenous being reinforces the structures that have caused its injury (see also Brown 1995). In making subjects responsible for changing themselves, the political choices made by the world that set the conditions for the lives of the subjects recede from view. The unwillingness of neoliberal politics to treat the past and present conditions of indigeneity as political issues in their own right—conditions that to this day urge fundamental political, legal and social change—amounts to a depoliticization of those conditions.

A prominent tool for diluting the politics in indigeneity, and its conditions, is the peoples' expected engagement in and commitment to the community. Much like the 'community-based healing' discourses in Canada starting from the 1990s (Coulthard 2014, p. 121), the contemporary resilience approach draws on an assumption of self-reliant communities coping with risks and uncertainties caused by the given conditions. The responsibilization of communities derives from a logic that uncertainty is a natural condition without any political purchase. Within this frame, the role of the governor is to provide support for the governed to build their capacities appropriately. Those being governed are guided toward the desired ways of living by support, not coercion and direct orders (see also Strakosch 2015).

Placing the responsibility on the indigenous subjects for healing their own wounds and trauma—both individually and as a community—denies any opportunities for politics on the basis of these injuries. It is as if politics does not see, or does not want to see, that the very question of indigenous peoples' injury is a question of/for politics. As a result of this reluctance to see and recognize the issue at hand, as Welsh (2014, p. 20) aptly notes, "there is little sign of a profound engagement with a politics of resilience as a means for conceiving of change; of revolution through resilience."

To be sure, there have been and continue to be attempts to compensate and 'correct' the conditions of the peoples. And indeed, one might view the interest expressed by states and in global politics in remedying the situation of indigenous peoples as an acknowledgment of their responsibility to 'do something' to improve the conditions of the peoples, to tackle the challenges involved and to eliminate the causes of their suffering. Indigenous peoples are seen as the ones who need to claim equal rights, state recognition, opportunities to participate, access to land and resources and, for example, self-determination. The underlying assumption is that the peoples lack these rights or entitlements. For example, the well-meaning idea of 'protecting, respecting and remedying' encouraged by the UN (Office of the High Commissioner for Human Rights 2011) suggests that indigenous peoples should receive some sort of compensation for the conditions caused, for example, by natural resource extraction. The adoption of the UNDRIP by the UN member states is also an effort to compensate the peoples for their losses and mistreatment. However, as Hale's (2005, p. 12) critical deconstruction of multiculturalism demonstrates, compensating "disadvantaged cultural groups" by granting collective rights fits in neatly with the neoliberal idea of cost-effectiveness. By offering watered-down remedies as evidence of colonial remorse, such as the UNDRIP (e.g. see Lightfoot 2012), hierarchical power relations are allowed to persist. Whether the half-hearted remedies are a consequence or cause of faded injustices (Alfred 2005; Coulthard 2014), the end result is a depoliticization of indigeneity and of its demands of the present order. The idea of compensation and remedy as such does not shake the fundamental structure on which politics rests.

The foregoing critical discussion on resilience indicates that the acts of assuaging colonial guilt strip indigeneity of its political potential. Offering remedies is a continuation of the neoliberal idea whereby resilient subjects and communities, despite their vulnerabilities, are to be autonomous, responsible and able to decide 'wisely'. On the basis of the injustices they have suffered, indigenous peoples reserve access and entitlement to political, legal and moral remedies. At the same time, this role of 'claimant' functions as a way to exclude indigeneity. Once their predicament is deemed remedied, the peoples are left to their own devices to cope. This "processes of remedial abandonment", as Mark Duffield (2011b, p. 763) has termed it, is part and parcel of the apparatus of resilience that insists on the subject's duty to cope with its conditions. For example, monetary compensation to indigenous peoples to organize social services that help overcome the trauma of being erased and denied a presence in what was—and still is—a colonial society has not, and will not, change the colonial set-up. The process of remedying is just a maneuver that marks indigenous peoples not as the ones who set the terms of change but as those who simply adjust, a move that saps indigeneity of its political potential.

On balance, what the resilience discourse of global politics has done is to replace references to victimhood with a vocabulary of adaptation and active agency. The term 'victim' is either not used or, when used, is played down. The acknowledgment of indigenous peoples being vulnerable is always coupled with their being capable of coping and responding. The victims of the past are today's active agents, who are recognized as vulnerable, yet possess an enormous capability to adapt and survive. In sum, the resilience approach, with its emphasis on the subject has, in the case of indigenous peoples, as Schott notes, reinforced the idea that "there is no unfinished business from the past or that such business puts no claims on the present" (Schott 2013, pp. 213–214). This is an idea that international politics has smoothly and effortlessly incorporated into its treatment of and proceedings with indigenous peoples. For indigenous peoples, who have more 'unfinished business' from the past than most, a politics that overlooks their victimhood and proffers adaptability and empowerment is a politics of violence. In fact, the active agency and adaptability urged by the resilience discourse are means by which the political in indigeneity is watered down and compromised, means wholly on par with remedying, responsibilizing communities and subjectifying colonial trauma.

References

Agrawal, Arun. 2005. *Environmentality. Technologies of Government and the Making of Subjects.* Durham: Duke University Press.

Alfred, Taiaiake. 2005. *Wasáse: Indigenous Pathways of Action and Freedom.* Peterborough: Broadview Press.

Arctic Climate Impact Assessment. 2005. Cambridge: Cambridge University Press.

Arctic Human Development Report. 2004. Akyreyri: Stefansson Arctic Institute.

Arctic Resilience Report. 2016. M. Carson and G. Peterson, eds. Stockholm Environment Institute and Stockholm Resilience Centre, Stockholm. https://oaarchive.arctic-council.org/handle/11374/1838. Accessed 21 June 2017.

Austin-Broos, Diane J., and Francesca Merlan, eds. 2017. *Peoples and Change in Indigenous Australia.* Honolulu: University of Hawaii Press.

Bastidas, Edith. 2008. Presenting the Declaration of the Preparatory Meeting for the 7th session of the UN PF, held 3–4 April 2008 in Santa Cruz de la Sierra, Bolivia. 22 April. Statements are available at the DoCip website. https://www.docip.org/en/indigenous-peoples-at-the-un/permanent-forum. Accessed 4 June 2017.

Brigg, Morgan. 2007. Biopolitics Meets Terrapolitics: Political Ontologies and Governance in Settler-Colonial Australia. *Australian Journal of Political Science* 42 (3): 403–417.

Brown, Wendy. 1995. *States of Injury: Power and Freedom in Late Modernity.* Princeton: Princeton University Press.

Butler, Judith, and Athena Athanasiou. 2013. *Dispossession: The Performative in the Political.* Cambridge: Polity Press.

Caron, Fred. 2008. Assistant Deputy Minister, Observer Delegation of Canada. Statement at the 7th session of the Permanent Forum. Statements are available at the DoCip website. https://www.docip.org/en/indigenous-peoples-at-the-un/permanent-forum. Accessed 4 June 2017.

Chandler, David, and Jon Coaffee, eds. 2017. *The Routledge Handbook of International Resilience.* London: Routledge.

Chandler, David, and Julian Reid. 2016. *The Neoliberal Subject. Resilience, Adaptation and Vulnerability.* London: Rowman & Littlefield.

Collis, Paul, and Jen Webb. 2014. The Visible and the Invisible: Legacies of Violence in Contemporary Australian Aboriginal Contexts. *Journal of Australian Studies* 38 (4): 490–503.

Corntassel, Jeff. 2012. Re-envisioning Resurgence. Indigenous Pathways to Decolonization and Sustainable Self-Determination. *Decolonization: Indigeneity, Education & Society* 1 (1): 86–101.

Coulthard, Glen Sean. 2014. *Red Skin, White Masks. Rejecting the Colonial Politics of Recognition.* Minneapolis: University of Minnesota Press.

Dillon, Michael. 2005. Cared to Death. The Biopoliticised Time of Your Life. *Foucault Studies* 2: 37–46.

Drichel, Simone. 2013. Reframing Vulnerability: 'So Obviously the Problem…'? *SubStance* 42 (3): 3–27. http://sub.uwpress.org/content/42/3/3.full.pdf+html. Accessed 21 June 2017.

Duffield, Mark. 2011a. *Environmental Terror: Uncertainty, Resilience and the Bunker* (Working Paper No. 06-11). http://www.bristol.ac.uk/media-library/sites/spais/migrated/documents/duffield-0611.pdf. Accessed 4 July 2017.

———. 2011b. Total War as Environmental Terror: Linking Liberalism, Resilience, and the Bunker. *South Atlantic Quarterly* 110: 757–769.

Evans, Brad, and Julian Reid. 2014. *Resilient Life. The Art of Living Dangerously.* Cambridge: Polity.

Forbes, Bruce C. 2013. Cultural Resilience of Social-Ecological Systems in the Nenets and Yamal-Nenets Autonomous Okrugs, Russia: A Focus on Reindeer Nomads of the Tundra. *Ecology and Society* 18 (4): 36.

Furedi, Frank. 2008. Fear and Security: A Vulnerability-led Policy Response. *Social Policy & Administration* 42 (6): 645–661.

Hale, Charles R. 2005. Neoliberal Multiculturalism: The Remaking of Cultural Rights and Racial Dominance in Central America. *PoLAR: Political and Legal Anthropology Review* 28 (1): 10–28.

Hovelsrud, Grete K., and Barry Smit, eds. 2010. *Community Adaptation and Vulnerability in Arctic Regions.* London: Springer.

Indigenous Caucus. 2002. Statement on Economic and Social Development. 2nd Session of the Permanent Forum on Indigenous Issues, 11–23 May. Statements are available at the DoCip website. https://www.docip.org/en/indigenous-peoples-at-the-un/permanent-forum/. Accessed 4 June 2017.

Joseph, Jonathan. 2012. *The Social in the Global. Social Theory, Governmentality and Global Politics.* Cambridge: Cambridge University Press.

———. 2013. Resilience as Embedded Neoliberalism: A Governmentality Approach. *Resilience: International Policies, Practices and Discourses* 1 (1): 38–52.

Lightfoot, Sheryl. 2012. Selective Endorsement without Intent to Implement: Indigenous Rights and the Anglosphere. *The International Journal of Human Rights* 16 (1): 100–122.

Lindroth, Marjo, and Heidi Sinevaara-Niskanen. 2013. At the Crossroads of Autonomy and Essentialism: Indigenous Peoples in International Environmental Politics. *International Political Sociology* 7 (3): 275–293.

———. 2014. Adapt or Die? The Biopolitics of Indigeneity—From the Civilising Mission to the Need for Adaptation. *Global Society* 28 (2): 180–194.

———. 2016. The Biopolitics of Resilient Indigeneity and the Radical Gamble of Resistance. *Resilience: International Policies, Practices and Discourses* 4 (2): 130–145.

MacDonald, Henry. 2008. Permanent Representative of Suriname to the United Nations. 7th session of the UN Permanent Forum. Statements are available at the DoCip website. https://www.docip.org/en/indigenous-peoples-at-the-un/permanent-forum/. Accessed 4 June 2017.

Magga, Ole-Henrik. 2002. Chairperson of the Permanent Forum. 1st Session of the Permanent Forum. May 12. Statements are available at the DoCip website. https://www.docip.org/en/indigenous-peoples-at-the-un/permanent-forum/. Accessed 4 June 2017.

Neumann, Iver B., and Ole Jacob Sending. 2010. *Governing the Global Polity: Practice, Mentality, Rationality.* Ann Arbor: The University of Michigan Press.

O'Malley, Pat. 1996. Indigenous Governance. *Economy and Society* 25 (3): 310–326.

Office of the High Commissioner for Human Rights. 2011. *Guiding Principles for Business and Human Rights: Implementing the United Nations "Protect, Respect and Remedy" Framework.* http://www.ohchr.org/Documents/Publications/GuidingPrinciplesBusinessHR_EN.pdf. Accessed 4 June 2017.

Olsson, Gunilla. 2008. Executive Director. International Fund for Agricultural Development (IFAD). 21 April. Statement at the 7th session of the Permanent Forum. Statements are available at the DoCip website. https://www.docip.org/en/indigenous-peoples-at-the-un/permanent-forum/. Accessed 4 June 2017.

Reid, Julian. 2012. The Disastrous and Politically Debased Subject of Resilience. *Development Dialogue* 58: 67–80.

Reidy, Trisha. 2008. United Nations Institute for Training and Research (UNITAR). Statement at the 7th session of the Permanent Forum. Statements are available at the DoCip website. https://www.docip.org/en/indigenous-peoples-at-the-un/permanent-forum/. Accessed 2 June 2017.

Rutherford, Stephanie. 2007. Green Governmentality: Insights and Opportunities in the Study of Nature's Rule. *Progress in Human Geography* 31 (3): 291–307.

Schott, Robin May. 2013. Resilience, Normativity and Vulnerability. *Resilience: International Policies, Practices and Discourses* 1 (3): 210–218.

Sejersen, Frank. 2015. *Rethinking Greenland and the Arctic in the Era of Climate Change. New Northern Horizons.* Abingdon: Routledge.

Sinevaara-Niskanen, Heidi. 2015. *Setting the Stage for Arctic Development: Politics of Knowledge and the Power of Presence.* Rovaniemi: Lapland University Press.

Sinevaara-Niskanen, Heidi, and Monica Tennberg. 2012. Responsibilisation for Adaptation. In *Governing the Uncertain: Adaptation and Climate in Russia and Finland*, ed. Monica Tennberg, 125–136. London: Springer.

Strakosch, Elizabeth. 2015. *Neoliberal Indigenous Policy: Settler Colonialism and the 'Post-Welfare' State.* London: Palgrave Macmillan.

Summerville, Jennifer A., Barbara A. Adkins, and Gavin Kendall. 2008. Community Participation, Rights, and Responsibilities: The Governmentality of Sustainable Development Policy in Australia. *Environment and Planning C: Government and Policy* 26 (4): 696–711.

Tennberg, Monica. 2009. Three Spirals of Power/Knowledge: Scientific Laboratories, Environmental Panopticons and Emerging Biopolitics. In *Legacies and Change in Polar Science. Historical, Legal and Political Reflections on the International Polar Year*, ed. Jessica M. Shadian and Monica Tennberg, 189–200. Surrey: Ashgate.

Thisted, Kirsten. 2013. Discourses of Indigeneity: Branding Greenland in the Age of Self-Government and Climate Change. In *Science, Geopolitics and Culture and in the Polar Region: Norden Beyond Borders*, ed. Sverker Sörlin, 227–258. Farnham: Ashgate.

UNESCO. 2012. *Weathering Uncertainty. Traditional Knowledge for Climate Change Assessment and Adaptation.* http://unesdoc.unesco.org/images/0021/002166/216613e.pdf. Accessed 20 Mar 2017.

Walker, Jeremy, and Melinda Cooper. 2011. Genealogies of Resilience: From Systems Ecology to the Political Economy of Crisis Adaptation. *Security Dialogue* 42: 143–160.

Welsh, Marc. 2014. Resilience and Responsibility: Governing Uncertainty in a Complex World. *The Geographical Journal* 80 (1): 15–26.

World Economic and Social Survey. 2016. *Climate Change Resilience: An Opportunity for Reducing Inequalities.* Department of Economic and Social Affairs, United Nations Secretariat. https://wess.un.org/wp-content/uploads/2016/06/WESS_2016_Report.pdf. Accessed 8 Feb 2017.

CHAPTER 5

Modes of Love

Biopolitical Love

As resilience has become to epitomize indigeneity in institutions, such as the Arctic Council and the UN, as well as in the common perceptions of indigeneity, it has become more important to tap the new modes of power operating in global politics. The increasingly prominent 'resilience' discourse (Joseph 2013; Welsh 2013; Evans and Reid 2014) resonates with biopolitical aspirations to govern indigenous lives. As resilience has become a pervasive concept and condition in relation to indigeneity, deconstructing it is crucial if we are to understand the limitless power trained on indigenous peoples.

Neoliberal politics, in particular, is an exercise of 'vital politics' (Lemke 2011), one that governs subjectivities and populations in the name of care. This 'biopolitics' has its premises and aspirations in the care of all life "for the sake of all life" (Prozorov 2007, p. 56). Through biopolitics, life is administered and improved and, if necessary, life's undesirable elements are eliminated (Foucault 1978; Ojakangas 2005; Reid 2006; Campbell and Sitze 2013; Dean 2013). The coercive force exercised over people has morphed to caring modes of exercising power that, instead of brutally ordering subjects to act and behave in a certain way, suggest 'suitable' solutions and persuade subjects in an empathetic manner. If historically the interventions in human lives were made in the name of order and discipline, today they are justified in the name of empathy. Biopolitics

M. Lindroth, H. Sinevaara-Niskanen, *Global Politics and Its Violent Care for Indigeneity*,
https://doi.org/10.1007/978-3-319-60982-9_5

narrates itself as a form of care, one operationalized 'for your good' and with the 'best of intentions'. It is only with good in mind that subjects are encouraged to live their lives and perform their humanity in a particular way at each given time, regardless of whether the subjectivity at work is a resilient, entrepreneurial or empowered one. This shift from an oppressive and limiting rationality of governing to power that appears in caring and loving modes is demonstrably present in the ways in which indigenous peoples have been treated.

The continuous concern over indigeneity is a deeply historical phenomenon, and the interventions made in the name of guiding indigenous peoples have varied. The impetus for interventions has, however, been rooted in necessity: the caring father has no other choice but to discipline his offspring in order for them to grow up 'proper'. Early colonial power took the form of a paternal educator demanding a certain kind of indigenous subjectivity and promising "salvation and civilisation" in turn (Morgensen 2011, p. 62). At the core of this paternal power was the aim of forcefully guiding indigenous peoples physically and culturally to alter and improve their bodies, practices and beliefs. In the colonial era, the disciplining of indigenous lives to make them 'proper' relied on corporeal politics, a politics that went into the substance of the indigenous being very concretely (e.g. Hale 2002; Scott 2005; Morgensen 2011). This corporeal colonialism, as Sylvester (2006, p. 68) describes it, forced people:

> [...] to cover their bodies, subject their bodies to hygiene, fill their bodies with western knowledge, move their bodies to different lands, use their bodies for slave and wage labour, and fight other bodies in the name of the colonizing state... Bodies that seemed too "other" to fit on the approved colonized/development line could suffer assault and death...

Historically, the capacity of the indigenous subject to adapt to given conditions literally marked the line between surviving and perishing. Much as colonial atrocities were corporealized by the indigenous being, the physical and mental capacities that enabled the colonized to survive those atrocities had to be drawn from within the very bodies of the colonized themselves. The *bio* in the adaptability required by corporeal colonialism meant a vocal, visible and concrete disciplining of bodies and minds. Indigenous life was targeted as material by colonial rule.

While the brutality that extended to the flesh and blood of the colonized might have ceased, the underlying pastoral power, as Povinelli (2011, pp. 25–26) observes, still deems it necessary to guide indigenous peoples. To be sure, even though global politics today condemns violence toward indigenous peoples and seeks to safeguard their human rights, one still sees violence and hostility toward the peoples in local and national contexts. Stating here that the corporeal brutality of colonialism has given way to more subtle forms of power is not to ignore the seriousness of the situations and suffering that some of indigenous peoples face at this very moment. Our analysis of power and governing, which focuses on common ground of contemporary international politics, hinges on demonstrable changes in political practices and parlance. The benevolent parlance of international politics, as circulated by the UN and the Arctic Council, among other forums, might clash with the lived realities of many indigenous peoples. No matter how sugar-coated or airbrushed that parlance might be, global politics has as its common ground certain political, legal and moral norms that define what acceptable treatment of indigenous peoples is and what it is not. In the history of indigenous peoples and their human rights, this is a rather recent development.

The global political parlance has changed to reflect the developments in politics and the acceptable treatment of the peoples. However, the key to understanding contemporary colonialism is to not take these developments at face value or as sincere signs of progress. Whereas colonial brutality aimed at 'civilizing' the peoples by disciplining them to grow up 'proper' and, where they failed to do so, eradicating them, the underlying aims of current interventions, which claim to protect, are harder to discern. The paternal concern for indigeneity today not only values and celebrates but also nurtures the exceptionality of indigenous peoples, supposedly for the sake of their lives. International political measures, as discussed through the empirical cases of the United Nations and the Arctic Council, treasure indigeneity and foster capacities perceived as inherently indigenous. In our view, these measures are part and parcel of the governing of indigeneity, however well-meaning they may seem superficially. The global concern and interest of the international community in fostering a particular kind of indigeneity are precisely exponents of the forces that sustain colonial power; the emperor's biopolitical clothes have been sewn anew.

The concept of biopolitics has gained ground in analyses of historical and ongoing corporeal practices of colonialism (e.g. Inda 2005; Morgensen 2011; Cupples 2012). As we apply it in this book, biopolitics informs a theoretical approach that makes it possible to grasp the ways in which the contemporary governing of life succeeds in disciplining its subjects, even without direct bodily intervention. In this regard, our focus differs from that seen in studies on the disciplining of indigenous bodies in specific local settings. As we argue, indigenous peoples have become a specific collectivity to be governed globally. The peoples continue to be governed as 'populations', as in colonial times (Watson 2015, p. 95), but the ways in which this governing is executed have changed. Today, the neoliberal order, pursuing its particular ends, manages the indigenous peoples by fostering the aspects of indigenous life that are deemed desirable and ignoring those that are less so. As we argue, a biopolitical wave of colonialism has taken over.

Indeed, indigenous peoples, who have faced the brutal and violent actions of colonialism, now find themselves surrounded by recognition, acceptance and praise. Yet, despite its veneer of benevolence—nurture for indigenous lives and 'being'—and more subtle forms, the colonial grip is as violent as ever. As Prozorov (2007, p. 59; see also Dillon 2005 on micro-practices of biopower) has aptly put it, at the same time as caring biopolitics "disqualifies death from politics", it intervenes in human existence in a number of ways by "manipulating the life choices of the individual" and penetrating the most mundane areas of life. Indeed, in the contemporary power setting, life continues to be the "stuff of biopolitics" (Dillon 2005, p. 42). When life is perceived as 'material', its usefulness, desirability and/or disposability for the purposes of governing is rendered an object of assessment. This enables politics to take a stand on what kind of life is worth investing in. In Dillon's words (2005, p. 42; see also Evans and Reid 2014, on life to be authenticated and disqualified), this continuous assessment results in a determination that "some life will be found to be worth investment, some life less worth investment." While biopolitics pervades and governs all life, it affects indigenous lives in particular.

The supporting of indigenous life, the maximizing of its potential and the nurturing of what indigeneity is perceived to be—adaptive and resilient—play out in multiple and recurring political, legal and local practices. The fact that these certain understandings of indigenous peoples and indigeneity recur and that there are so few, if any, counter-representations mirrors the very existence of biopolitical order. These shared and uncontentious conceptions that recur rely on, expect and affirm a particular and distinguishable indigeneity, one that is 'exceptional', flexible, care-taking and resilient. The engagement of global politics in viewing indigeneity through these parameters amounts to a global commitment to treat indigeneity accordingly. What we see globally is a predisposition to indigeneity that is the object of continuous interventions in the name of care—care that wants to empower the traditional capacities of the peoples, support their resilience and build up their adaptability. Indeed, the call for resilient and ever-adapting indigeneity is very eye-catching in contemporary politics, but very little attention has been paid to the ways in which that call governs indigenous life. A critical reading of this call is conspicuous by its absence (for notable exceptions drawing on politics on the national level and indigenous endurance, see Brigg 2007; Povinelli 2011; Sutton 2009; Strakosch 2015).

The power of the current neoliberal politics that celebrates the resilience and adaptability of subjects lies in its overarching and tempting promise of care—care that is, ultimately, violent in nature. The benign and empathetic common ground on what indigeneity is supposed to be manifests the "loving embrace" of biopower (Prozorov 2007, p. 56). Power might have changed from being brutal to more subtle (Lindroth and Sinevaara-Niskanen 2014) and from being intimate to distant (Joseph 2013), but the aim of directing lives persists. Indeed, the ways in which governing is carried out have transitioned from submitting the flesh and mind of the subject to direct physical and mental commands to indirect and distant techniques that make the subject monitor, discipline and improve itself. The self-reliance and responsibility of the subject—whatever this may mean at any given time and in any given place—is a new form of ordering. The neoliberal rationality relies on these subjects, capable of and willing to transform themselves according to its rule. And it is with joy and enthusiasm that the neoliberal subject then engages in making itself more fit, healthy, active, empowered, educated and informed in order to thrive in its role as a member of the society (e.g. Larner and Walters 2004; Li 2007; Brown 2015).

Accordingly, the shared understandings of indigeneity foster and steer indigenous life by signaling what the indigenous subject should be like. Despite being conducted in a more subtle and a distant manner, in the end the management of indigeneity goes on. As Dillon (2005, p. 44) insightfully notes, "the promotion, protection and investment of the life of individuals and populations – elides the issue of being cared to death." The empathy of biopower perpetrates violence against indigeneity: it defines proper indigeneity and elements to be cast aside. Thus, the loving embrace of politics and law might mean slow suffocation (on unbearable and suffocating biopower, see Prozorov 2007, p. 59) for indigenous 'beings' who are disqualified as inauthentic. The selective inclusion of the peoples and their concerns in political and legal systems is a smoke screen that enables those systems to consciously turn a blind eye to certain features of indigenous lives. The types of indigeneity that are not recognized as authentic—those that are too urban, too modern and not distinguishable enough from the rest of us—inevitably fall by the wayside as regards political, legal and financial protection, benefits and support. The refusal to invest in indigeneity in its contemporary diversity and heterogeneity is tantamount to snuffing out the types of indigenous life not considered worthy of receiving the prerequisites for life.

As previous studies have also noted, it is difficult to pinpoint the practices of governing life exercised in the name of care and masked by its benevolent concern. In a biopolitical setting, where the governing of the subject means intervening in its very existence, way of living, life choices and day-to-day existence, the techniques by which these interventions work are myriad and subtle. That is precisely why biopolitical governing is so effective and, at the same time, so hard to detect. In order to grasp the larger logic of the biopolitics at work on indigeneity, we tease out three component practices of this power. As the techniques of governing life vary according to each given time, place and object, so, too, do the particular practices trained on indigeneity. The ways in which global politics governs indigenous being work, in particular, through the celebration of indigenous exceptionality, the (selective) recognition of indigenous rights and needs and the entanglement of indigeneity with long-term political, legal and economic processes that promise hope. The loving gaze of global politics that falls on indigeneity says 'I see you', 'I recognize your needs' and 'I want your best, so bear with me'. How could one resist such a tempting promise?

'I See You'

The legacy of colonialism is palpable in the ways in which indigeneity becomes visible or remains invisible. The process of acknowledging indigenous being in the colonial era, as Collis and Webb (2014, p. 495) aptly summarize it, was not a matter of failing to see the peoples and their (dis) possessions; rather it was a "conscious choice to see nothing, rather than the something that they [the settlers] knew was there". In a similar way, the empathetic politics of today is pregnant with a desire to view indigeneity in a particular way. This amounts to a refusal to see it as anything more or different than what the fantasy entertained by this politics allows. A caretaking, vulnerable, yet adaptive (and hence resilient) subjectivity is the contemporary incarnation of indigeneity. This partial, incomplete, essentialized and dichotomous perception of indigeneity is what underpins the exercise of biopolitical power over indigenous lives.

What makes the biopower trained on indigenous peoples particular is, first, the continuation and renewal of measures that are directed at indigenous being and, second, the ways in which these measures are contradictory. The features that defined indigenous peoples as 'savages' before—for example, their intimate relationship with nature, traditional knowledge and practices and living off the land—are the very features that are now invoked and celebrated. To be sure, the brutality of past measures lingers in indigenous lives, for example, in the form of languages and cultural legacies lost. However, in the neoliberal setting of subjects struggling to survive the insecurity of the world, it is, ironically, the very features and abilities of the peoples to cope, adapt and survive that form the premises for the (mis) recognition of indigeneity. The very features that once put them into the colonial category of 'savages' are now used to lift them up onto a pedestal and celebrate them as potential saviors of humanity. For example, the hype over indigenous adaptability entails a colonial pattern whereby indigenous peoples are the ones who must adapt to existing and forthcoming conditions. At the same time, an adaptive subjectivity and being is required for indigeneity to be recognized by contemporary politics. The peoples must sustain and reproduce their authenticity and distinctiveness as adaptive and resilient subjects in order to gain recognition and become entitled to certain rights and positions. Trying to fulfill this fantasy is the contemporary "indefinite detention" of indigeneity, an expression coined by Butler (2004, p. 67), that we find most appropriate for present purposes as well. To become visible in the eyes of politics and law, indigeneity needs to nurse, (re)produce and guard its exceptionality, the sole basis on which it comes into being.

At the same time, recognizing indigeneity as no more than resilience and adaptability draws a line between indigenous life to be validated and worth investing in and that to be disqualified. The quest for resilient subjects, indigenous and others involves "inculcating particular subjectivities that are fit for purpose" in the face of a world of contingency (Welsh 2013, p. 5). Resilient indigeneity differs from the resilience expected of others in that being alert, accommodating and flexible are allegedly qualities that the peoples possess at birth and can thus readily operationalize and harness. This idea of indigenous peoples being injured, yet performing as resilient subjects by displaying the capacity to claim their rights on the basis of that injury, is also embedded in international law (see also Birrell 2016). In order to appear in politics and before the law, indigeneity is required to be distinctive and recognizable. As things stand, indigeneity cannot argue for rights and protection without highlighting and assuring that such distinctiveness and/or distinction exists.

The basis for this distinctiveness and separateness is formed on the terms set by others, not the peoples themselves. The distinctiveness that indigeneity is expected to conform to is not that of indigeneity in all its variety but of a stereotypical indigeneity that differs from Western parameters. To bind indigeneity to distinctiveness is a conscious choice that glosses over the fact that in many instances—coping with changing environments, sustaining local communities or making individual life choices—the similarity of what are considered 'indigenous' and 'Western' lives should be deemed the defining feature. Thus, the bounded presence of indigenous being is encapsulated in the political and legal desire to nurture and care exclusively for the type of indigeneity that is properly separate (on distinctiveness and law, see also Butler 2004, pp. 24–25).

Indeed, there is a cumulative process of seeing indigeneity through a certain prism. For indigenous peoples, this means performing their indigeneity and appearing in the ways valorized by this prism instead of emphasizing features grounded in something other than the relations between indigenous and other peoples (Merlan 2009, p. 305). While such a distinctiveness might exist, the twist in the current political and legal care for indigeneity is that there is no alternative other than indigenous peoples settling for, embracing and reproducing their exceptionality. If they do not succeed in this, they risk being deemed inauthentic and thus not eligible for the entitlements attached to indigeneity (Sissons 1997, p. 32). As Butler and Athanasiou (2013, p. 76) critically observe:

> In this particular context [recognition], where national ideological formation of multiculturalism becomes the grounds for new national monoculturalism, Indigenous subjects are called on to perform an authentic self-identity of prenational, "traditional" cultural difference ... as the grounds for a viable or felicitous native title claim and in exchange for the nation's recognition and the states reparative legislation.

The requirement of exceptionality, which one might consider merely a prerequisite for politics and law to operate in practice, in fact, touches the very core of indigenous existence.

Performing exceptionality successfully is not only a matter of becoming entitled to enter global politics or gaining access to land (e.g. Knafla and Westra 2010) but—perhaps even more so—a matter of subjects struggling to perform their identity in a recognizable way. The promise of progress and rights, as well as the cultural distinctiveness seen as a precondition for them, has put pressure on local communities to define who is indigenous. As a result, the well-meaning care for indigeneity has engendered local disagreement and divisions. For example, the two-decade-long discussion about the ratification of ILO Convention No. 169 which would recognize the rights of the Saami people to their land in Finland, has sparked debates on who is a Saami, with these then leading to a fracturing of local communities (on discussions on who is a Saami, see, for example, Joona 2015; Valkonen et al. 2017). The struggle to prove one's identity as a Saami is for many an emotionally trying and intimate process as one's identification with the groups and culture may have been undermined, questioned and even denied.

In sum, exceptionality becomes a naturalized norm to which the indigenous peoples must adapt. What this exceptionality accomplishes is to regulate indigenous subjects and their existence biopolitically: assumptions of exceptionality (Brigg 2007; see also Lindroth and Sinevaara-Niskanen 2013) and peculiarity (Rifkin 2009, p. 112) serve to construct subjectivities and justify interventions in indigenous lives. The indigenous life promoted and considered fit for the purpose is a life that must significantly differ from that of the Western, urban, industrialized and individualized world. As Butler and Athanasiou (2013, p. 76) have noted in their discussion on dispossession, there is a "'difference' that liberalism loves to tolerate". In the case of indigeneity, the politically, legally and socially tolerable differences are the type of differences that do not offend or repulse. Indigeneity is expected to be different, but within such limits as keep it exotically appealing and transferable to Western imaginaries. For example, the role ascribed to indigenous peoples as care-takers of the environment—the impetus for invoking their particular knowledge—is considered worthy and important as long as it does not clash with prevailing ideas on the use and role of the environment. The entire idea of traditional ecological knowledge being merged with Western science and knowledge signals that indigeneity, as well as the features that supposedly set it apart from the rest of us, must be translatable to the Western understanding of it. As such, the tolerated difference means that indigeneity is not to be too 'primitive'. Features that are 'too much' or 'not enough' are ignored.

Povinelli (2011) as well notes that the difference that is loved has its limits. There are limits beyond which liberal recognition turns away from "its supposed commitment to valuing the diversity of the other" and refuses to tolerate and recognize such a difference (Povinelli 2011, p. 80). The fact that there is such a fine line between being the one cared for and the one that is not tolerated, and that the shift from unwanted to loved has, in historical perspective, happened almost overnight, offers a glimpse into the workings of current biopolitical control over the indigenous peoples. The difference and otherness that indigeneity is deemed to represent is, in Alfred's (2005, p. 126) words, one of the colonial "identity inventions" that are used "to dispossess and assimilate". Biopolitical love, which sees indigeneity in a particular light, only shows affection for what it desires in indigeneity. This love is fickle: as long as indigeneity corresponds to the fantasy of proper difference, it celebrates and nurtures, but its care is not unconditional. If indigeneity does not meet the expectations placed on it, the violent care of contemporary biopolitics will allow the undesirable aspects of indigeneity to die.

'I Recognize Your Needs'

Instead of concluding that the intensifying discussion on the recognition of indigenous peoples and their rights signals a shift in power, we argue that the seemingly reorganized relations between states and indigenous peoples are signs of biopower at work. The benevolent aim of states and the international community to recognize indigenous peoples' rights is an attempt to redeem themselves for the mistreatment of the peoples. What is inscribed in this liberal recognition paradigm is that recognition is an answer and a solution to the wrongdoings that the indigenous peoples have suffered. Within this paradigm, the guiding idea is that indigenous peoples need and want political partnership, seats at the same table and 'slots' of their own within Western legal and political frameworks. The lines of recognition for indigeneity and indigenous subjects are sketched through the lens of exceptionality; indigeneity and its needs are determined and treated accordingly. The requirements of recognizability and cultural cohesiveness are among the key conditions for indigenous subjectivity to enter the processes of recognition. Whether the focal issue is entering the arenas of international politics or struggling for their lands in national contexts, the peoples have the burden of proof as regards their injury, connections to land, previous generations and cultural practices. As discussed earlier, their distinctiveness needs to be clear; the present beliefs, desires and hopes of the peoples must be connected "to the beliefs, desires and hopes of their pre-colonial ancestors" (Povinelli 2006, pp. 227–228).

What the process of recognition expects is that indigenous subjects possess a coherent 'pre-nation' identity and a visibly and tangibly authentic culture. The parameters for what qualifies as distinguishable and 'authentic' are set by the political and legal frames of the states in question. Indeed, recognition is built on the idea that the authority granting the recognition is "to demarcate intelligibility, to publicly institute and normalise the relatedness that matters" (Butler and Athanasiou 2013, p. 79). In sum, the indigenous subject needs to be different in ways that are at once recognizable and tolerable. The critical question raised, however, is how much and what kind of difference is acceptable. To what extent must indigeneity conform to and fulfill the fantasies that the recognition process has for indigenous traditionality and authenticity?

As indigeneity is seen merely as a particular type of being, the recognition of what that 'being' needs, requires and wants is also conditional on the idea(l) of such distinctive otherness. What follows from the current biopolitical care for particular indigenous lives is the predetermined set of legal and political maneuvers that are designed to cater to the needs of that particular fantasized subject. The 'seeing' of indigeneity—in law, politics and society at large—thus already entails an understanding and statement of what it is that indigeneity needs. In recognizing the exceptional needs of this exceptional subject, the recognition framework is wholly geared to the governing of indigenous lives biopolitically.

The recognition of indigenous rights has been seen as unavoidable progress that follows from the wrongdoings of history—a necessity, something that has to happen. Indeed, as Simpson (2014, p. 20) points out, recognition "appears as a transcendent and universal human desire" and as such is something that would seem to be able to repair the wounds of the past, both for the colonized and the colonizer. In the midst of recognition, portrayed as a promise, an end to colonialism and source of salvation, the conditions of that recognition are left unasked and unquestioned (see also Butler and Athanasiou 2013, p. 79). Recognition promises a change and a solution once and for all, but its premises remain as they always have been. Recognition is something that one cannot want; it is not to be tampered with. The mindset of recognition is, as Alfred (2005, p. 138) puts it succinctly, that indigenous cultures are to become amenable to the expectations of what they are supposed to be in order for states to recognize them and to make amends "for 'historical' injustices against those reimagined". Again, the care for indigenous peoples, performed in the form of recognition, is attuned to the fantasy of peculiar otherness.

As Povinelli (2011, p. 92) notes with insight, the indigenous being and otherness envisaged in the process of recognition, are not, however, mere fantasies but acts that enhance the kind of life, being or subjectivity worth of investing in and take a stance on what are the lives that do not count. She (2006, p. 54) has called this process of offering recognition—which is fundamentally misrecognition, but proffered as salvation for the deprived—"the cunning of recognition". The cunning of recognition has transformed

> [...] the discourse of demand into a discourse of recognition – ...the demand that [one has]... specific kind of knowledge... and a specific propositional attitude toward it if... [one] is to be recognized as a 'traditional Aboriginal subject'. (Povinelli 2006, p. 54)

Offering legal and political recognition that is conditional on the types of being that indigeneity is assumed to represent betokens the essentially unequal set-up of power exercised over indigeneity.

While it may seem that politics recognizes the needs of the indigenous peoples, by taking note of their dispossession in order to overcome that very same condition of deprivation, it is in fact a well-honed apparatus for the reproduction of dispossessed subjects. Recognition is a process that presumes one who lacks equal rights or has suffered injustices, one who is dispossessed. At the same time, the process of recognition itself—one requiring the subject to provide evidence of its deprivation and suffering—forces the subject to lock its identity to injury and to hold on to, not to abandon, its dispossessed existence. As Butler and Athanasiou (2013, pp. 1–2) note in this vein, crafting dispossession as a particular aspect of certain types of subjectivities amounts to making persons objects of "normative and normalizing powers that define cultural intelligibility and that regulate the distribution of vulnerability." The recognition of indigenous subjects and their needs on the basis of their injury and woundedness creates a situation where indigeneity cannot escape its permanent state of dispossession within the current political and legal liberal regime.

The violence of the care for indigeneity manifests itself in a recognition process based on misrecognition, and in the condition that if they are to gain any recognition—be it legal, political or social—the peoples need to conform to that misrecognition. The biopolitical grip on indigenous being is tight as the bases on which the peoples justify and argue for their subjectivity to be seen and recognized are very limited. As we cannot find better words to summarize the prices to be paid, the sacrifice to be made, for even the most basic forms of recognition no matter what one chooses from the available paths of recognition, we use Povinelli's. She speaks of dehumanization:

> In short... either love through liberal ideas of self-sovereignty and de-culture yourself, or love according to the fantasy of the unchanging dictates of your tradition and dehumanize yourself. (Povinelli 2006, pp. 227–228)

For indigeneity, gaining recognition involves both accommodating one's culture to the imposed liberal political and legal paradigm—de-culturing oneself—and conforming to the imaginaries of traditionality, exceptionality and distinctiveness, dehumanizing oneself. As we have noted, in order to argue for rights and recognition in global politics, indigeneity must fulfill the fantasy of peculiar otherness. Compliance with the fantasy of that politics, that is, accepting dehumanization, is a requirement for entering law and politics and performing before their respective powers-that-be. What results is, inevitably, de-culturation. As it stands, within this paradigm, indigeneity cannot be all that it is or might be. It is never welcomed as a whole, with its varied nuances, inconsistences and unconventionalities.

'I Want Your Best, So Bear with Me'

As components of biopolitical care, the process of recognition and the power setting that underpins it are pervasive and relentless. What defines this biopolitical care is not only (mis)recognition and the conditions set for it, but the fact that recognition is only a promise, one whose fulfillment keeps being postponed. Even though the peoples might be inclined to claim and settle for political, legal and social recognition—however partial—proposed by the states and the global community, this does not necessarily translate into their gaining that recognition, as history has demonstrated. The willingness of international politics to recognize the needs of the peoples entails an understanding of that politics as wanting the best for the peoples but, at the same time, pleading for their patience as granting recognition (allegedly) is a process fraught with complexities. The evolution of the UN Permanent Forum and the Arctic Council and the adoption of the UNDRIP are telling examples of the ways in which indigenous peoples have been asked to hold on, wait for better things to come and to trust that progress will eventually take place.

This is not to say that institutional developments in the UN and the Arctic Council have not taken place, but what, if anything, has been altered by changing the organizational charts? For indigenous peoples, despite their political inclusion and active engagement, eventual recognition and full achievement of their collective land and self-determination rights still hinges on external authorities setting the conditions for recognition and, ultimately, granting it. It is this uneven power setting that, it is assumed, indigeneity will accommodate itself to and endure. Indigenous peoples' demands for rights place them in political, legal and social 'waiting rooms', as Povinelli (2011) calls them, where the realization of their rights is suspended for the time being, but a hope is sustained that someday that realization will occur.

The promise of recognition and the idea(l) that politics cares for indigeneity engender hope that manifests itself in different ways. For example, in cases where indigenous peoples have claimed their rights, hope drives the peoples' efforts to regain what has historically belonged to them. The hope of finding the evidence required to prove possession of lands has sparked their struggle and maintains it. For example, even though there is no guarantee of success, hope—and the potential for change it evokes—has prompted the peoples in Fiji to go through the historical archives again and again (Miyazaki 2004). In some cases, the hope linked to progress and recognition has been engineered by the state in a very corporeal manner. In Mexico, for example, peasants have been given hope that their land claims will be resolved in order to discourage them from engaging in what the state considers illegal means of seeking justice. Resistance to such dictated hope or refusal to trust in the righteousness of the state's legal institutions has been met with violent punishment (Nuijten 2004, p. 227). Particularly in midst of current economic and social crises, hope is what is on offer for those seeking better circumstances, justice and equality (e.g. Appadurai 2013; Kleist and Jansen 2016).

Certainly, without hope and the action it engenders, indigenous peoples would not even have had a chance to secure the rights they now have. However, the unjust biopolitical flipside of hope and hopefulness is that despair is not an option; the peoples need to rely on the carefully crafted promises fed to them by neoliberal politics and law. In the neoliberal order and era of biopolitical governing, individuals and communities are made responsible for the realization of their rights. The violence of this setting is that those least responsible for their dispossession are now those that need to hope and harness their hopefulness to provide their strength and capacity they need to pursue their rights. As such, indigenous peoples being positioned such that they need to bear with and sustain hope entail a mindset that by harnessing their hopefulness, they can move on. At the same time, those responsible for the unequal setting in the first place are relieved from accountability.

The celebration of indigenous peoples and their inclusion in international politics is part of the same promise of a more just and equal future. Hope has been a defining feature of the establishment of both the UN Permanent Forum and the Arctic Council; hopes have been voiced that indigenous peoples will get an equal footing with the states, that their livelihoods and cultures will be protected, that the past injustices will be addressed and that the peoples will gain political, legal and moral leverage and, eventually, self-determination. This joyful inclusion in global politics has served the peoples hope on a silver platter. Notably, after 20 years, both of these political forums, despite their grand promises, continue to have little to offer indigenous peoples but hope. The fundamental promises remain unfulfilled: indigenous peoples are still marginalized; their cultures and livelihoods are suppressed; and their rights are either unrecognized or violated. The very same issues that featured on the agendas in the early days of the UN Permanent Forum and the Arctic Council remain on the agendas today. As the UN 2030 Agenda for Sustainable Development promises, no one is to be left behind and the most marginalized will be reached first (Transforming our World: the 2030 Agenda for Sustainable Development 2015). For the time being, however, global politics has offered the indigenous peoples mere words of welcome and a warm handshake instead of concrete acts of justice—be the issue returning lands and the profits gained from them or restoring the peoples' sovereign status as nations.

If paternal discipline could describe the treatment of indigenous peoples in international politics in the past, one could speak of parental care today. The way in which global politics has taken indigenous peoples under its wing as vulnerable ones resembles the care of parents toward their children. Whereas a strict father wanting the best for his children might have physically and mentally punished them to make them act as he wanted, the caring parents of today's world encourage certain behavior by promising rewards. Parental love allows some measure of freedom and choice, but the child is only allowed certain choices. At the same time, he or she has to bear the responsibility for the choices made. Similarly, international politics offers limited choices, all cloaked in 'good', to indigenous peoples. Inclusion, active participation and engagement in international politics are presented as ways to secure the fulfillment of the peoples' hopes for better and more equal treatment. The need for the peoples to claim recognition of their rights is presented as the preferred 'choice'. If the peoples—like children who are considered to be oblivious to their own good—should refuse the choice of partnership and inclusion and abandon Western political forums as avenues for regaining their self-determination, they will be left to their own devices to cope. In the midst of the loving parental care of global politics, the peoples are to understand the options offered and proffered as good and appropriate and to recognize the responsibilities, gains and losses involved.

Refusal of the loving care of biopower is "a radical gamble" (Prozorov 2007), that is, one in which the gains and losses are impossible to assess beforehand. As the investment of biopower in one's life is made in an empathetic, concerned and intimate manner, for indigenous peoples, a refusal to respond to the loving concerns of global politics that urge partnership and inclusion would put them at risk of losing what little voice, visibility and influence they now have. In heeding the call, as it were, what the peoples might gain in political access, they stand to lose in self-determination. Should they reject the ruling political system—structures imposed by the colonizer—they would be able to set their own agendas, but could lose the political recognition of states. Alfred (2005), Corntassel (2012) and Coulthard (2008), among others, have argued that this latter cause of action is the only option if indigenous peoples are to live their lives not determined by the colonial system. They suggest indigenous resurgence as an alternative avenue to the reactive resistance to or complying with the dominant political setting.

At the core of the parental care for indigeneity in international politics today is the expectation that the peoples are to bear with that politics; being patient is a necessary virtue of indigenous subjects. The expectation to "*persist* in potentiality", as Povinelli observes (2011, p. 128), is ascribed to indigeneity in particular. The fact that indigenous peoples in international politics have been promised something better and their hopes have been encouraged is part of the current colonial rationality, where power is exercised by generating promises whose fulfillment looms on the horizon but is never at hand. In such a process, where one is encouraged in a loving manner to persevere endlessly, one can, indeed, end up being "cared to death" (Dillon 2005). The care for indigeneity that international politics has shown to date has positioned indigeneity to wait and to be patient. The promise of progress and better things to come has yet to be redeemed and, as always, "the evidence [of things turning for the better] will not be in for quite some time" (Povinelli 2011, p. 191). Global politics insisting, through its practices, structures and rhetoric, that indigeneity is to persist in this state of potentiality—an expectation and a requirement only applicable to some—marks an exercise of colonial power through loving modes of biopower.

Eternally In-Between

The component practices of biopower that see indigeneity in terms of exceptionality attach the recognition of its rights to that exceptionality and, in the end, offer no more than promises that keep indigeneity hoping and waiting for their redemption. These three components of 'seeing', '(mis)recognizing' and 'pleading for patience' are transformed continuations of the power that has always been at work on indigeneity. What is at stake in this current assemblage of biopower that operates through seemingly benevolent care is indigenous subjectivity itself. Despite the acknowledgment that there is still a great deal to be done in improving the social, legal, political, economic and environmental conditions of the peoples, biopolitical care focuses on the struggling yet surviving subject. It is resilient, ever-adapting and malleable indigeneity that will yield the resources needed to endure and ultimately (and allegedly) to alter conditions. The signals of hope, as well as the encouragement to hold on, to be resilient and persevere, contribute to the realignment that is detaching subjects from their very conditions. Presumably, it is the subjects, even though they are not responsible for their deprivation and dispossession, who are the 'solution' to addressing, tackling and even 'fixing' these conditions. In this biopolitical setting, the very condition for the existence and survival of indigeneity is the particular indigenous subjectivity.

Indeed, what is crucial in the biopolitical modes of care is that they boil down to the subject. The tolerable recognizable difference and authenticity of the subject, the historical evidence of its dispossession and its engagement in the process that promises future redemption make the indigenous subject the focal point of global politics rather than justice, equality and correcting the wrongdoings of the past. Ordaining what kind of indigeneity is recognizable before the law and politics is to determine what is the indigeneity to be fostered and what is the indigeneity to be abandoned. Thus, processes of political and legal recognition are ultimately instances of policing. They are not concerned with acknowledging and redressing injustices and injuries, but rather function as apparatuses for governing subjects.

What is particular about this mode of biopolitical governing is that it places subjects in a process where they are eternally in the making and, as a result, always in-between. The subject worth investing in is one that strives to improve itself, enhances its adaptive capacities and cherishes its ability to cope on its own devices. In a word, it is a subject that is more resilient than it has ever been. Seemingly, the call for indigenous subjects who possess innate, enhanced and exceptional capacities stems from the inheritance of the past—a demonstrated ability to endure and survive even the harshest of conditions—and from the potential realization of rights and recognition in the future. However, as the fulfillment of future hopes constantly eludes them, indigenous subjects must remain responsive to the expectations and requirements imposed on their subjectivity if they are to keep that potential 'better' future on the horizon. Indigeneity is locked in a "temporal limbo" (Povinelli 2011, p. 78), "between the conditions of the past and the promise of the future". The rationality of 'bearing with' tells the peoples that "they will have to live with less now in order to live with more in future, or that their present deaths are actually a future redemption" (Povinelli 2011, p. 99). This in-betweenness is tantamount to a 'bracketing' of indigeneity, in which the peoples' existence and cause have been noted, but have been placed among the other issues to be resolved in the future. There is no telling when these brackets will be removed and if claims will be settled in the end.

In this limbo of potentiality and promise, the sources of salvation—as biopolitical care would have us believe—are the very capacities of the subjects themselves. For things to move on and improve, the subject is to be proactive, engaged and responsive. The debates on land rights are a prime legal and political avenue along which biopolitical care trickles down to the subjects. As is often the case, the recognition of such rights is suspended until it is determined who are entitled to the rights and all the consequences of those rights are clarified. In terms of those entitled to the potential rights, disputes arise over 'proper' ethnicity, and indigenous communities are often driven into identity struggles over how to perform ethnicity 'properly' and distinctively enough (e.g. Hale 2002; Sturm 2011; Birrell 2016). While communities are left to 'decide' for themselves who to include and exclude, those with the power to recognize the rights of the peoples can legitimately refuse to proceed or do anything at all for that matter. In order to move forward with their claims before such an authority, the peoples must represent a coherent 'we' that is convincing in its claim that it genuinely continues its cultural and historical distinctiveness. For example, a claim for native title in Australia requires the peoples not only to provide evidence of their genealogical past and connectedness to the land but to prove that there is an unbroken chain of cultural practices from past to present (e.g. Merlan 2016; Birrell 2016). Similarly, any messiness or uncertainty surrounding the consequences of the government recognizing Aboriginal rights functions as a valid reason for suspending their realization. Whether one considers the adoption of the UNDRIP at the UN General Assembly (e.g. Lightfoot 2012) or the ratification of ILO Convention No. 169 (e.g. Heinämäki et al. 2017), the uncharted political territory, that is, the recognition of the collective rights of indigenous peoples, daunts those in power, for the costs of realizing such rights are unknown. Clearly, it is a smart move for those in power to just say 'maybe', as this allows them to avoid the shame for not granting equal rights and recognition and the unease of not knowing what the potential results of granting such rights are. With that 'maybe' the responsibility for the struggle for rights and recognition and all that they entail is off-loaded onto the communities in question. Once again, what is called for is the coping, struggling, yet—in spite of everything—hopeful indigenous subject.

In terms of political subjectivity, what does this future projected in the promise of inclusion, rights and recognition entail? While politics offers them 'a place at the table' and equal rights—rights that are difficult not to want—the indigenous subject seeking recognition within the Western political and legal paradigm can never transform the power setting of this paradigm. The agreeable difference that indigeneity is called upon to present is no more than a felicitous and 'decorative' otherness that does not displease or fundamentally challenge the existing power setting. As a result, the indigeneity and indigenous subjectivity sought after in global politics has stagnated (Spivakovsky 2006), becoming an essentialized, romanticized and exotic otherness that leaves little room for indigenous subjects to influence or decide the course of political and legal events. For those assigned a seat in the waiting rooms of global politics—in as much as they have chosen to pursue the 'goods' promised by the liberal Western political system—there is no other choice than to follow a path that is marked by this system and to walk at the pace it sets. Coincidentally, the position that biopolitical care places indigeneity in denies indigenous subjects any possibility of radical change.

References

Alfred, Taiaiake. 2005. *Wasáse: Indigenous Pathways of Action and Freedom*. Peterborough: Broadview Press.

Appadurai, Arjun. 2013. *The Future as Cultural Fact. Essay on the Global Condition*. London: Verso.

Birrell, Kathleen. 2016. *Indigeneity: Before and Beyond the Law*. Abingdon: Routledge.

Brigg, Morgan. 2007. Biopolitics Meets Terrapolitics: Political Ontologies and Governance in Settler-Colonial Australia. *Australian Journal of Political Science* 42 (3): 403–417.

Brown, Wendy. 2015. *Undoing the Demos: Neoliberalism's Stealth Revolution*. New York: Zone Books.

Butler, Judith. 2004. *Precarious Life. The Powers of Mourning and Violence*. London: Verso.

Butler, Judith, and Athena Athanasiou. 2013. *Dispossession: The Performative in the Political*. Cambridge: Polity Press.

Campbell, Timothy, and Adam Sitze. 2013. Biopolitics: An Encounter. In *Biopolitics: A Reader*, ed. Timothy Campbell and Adam Sitze, 1–40. Durham: Duke University Press.

Collis, Paul, and Jen Webb. 2014. The Visible and the Invisible: Legacies of Violence in Contemporary Australian Aboriginal Contexts. *Journal of Australian Studies* 38 (4): 490–503.

Corntassel, Jeff. 2012. Re-envisioning Resurgence: Indigenous Pathways to Decolonization and Sustainable Self-Determination. *Decolonization: Indigeneity, Education & Society* 1 (1): 86–101.

Coulthard, Glen. 2008. Beyond Recognition: Indigenous Self-Determination as Prefigurative Practice. In *Lighting the Eighth Fire: The Liberation, Resurgence, and Protection of Indigenous Nations*, ed. Leanne Simpson, 187–203. Winnipeg: Arbeiter Ring Publishing.

Cupples, Julie. 2012. Wild Globalization: The Biopolitics of Climate Change and Global Capitalism on Nicaragua's Mosquito Coast. *Antipode* 44 (1): 10–30.

Dean, Mitchell. 2013. *The Signature of Power. Sovereignty, Governmentality and Biopolitics*. London: Sage.

Dillon, Michael. 2005. Cared to Death. The Biopoliticised Time of Your Life. *Foucault Studies* 2: 37–46.

Evans, Brad, and Julian Reid. 2014. *Resilient Life. The Art of Living Dangerously*. Cambridge: Polity Press.

Foucault, Michel. 1978. *The History of Sexuality: An Introduction*. London: Penguin.

Hale, Charles R. 2002. Does Multiculturalism Menace? Governance, Cultural Rights and the Politics of Identity in Guatemala. *Journal of Latin American Studies* 34 (3): 485–524.

Heinämäki, Leena, Christina Allard, Stefan Kirchner, Alexandra Xanthaki, Sanna Valkonen, Ulf Mörkenstam, Nigel Bankes, Jacinta Ruru, Jéremie Gilbert, Per Selle, Audra Simpson, and Laura Olsén. 2017. *Actualizing Sámi Rights: International Comparative Research*. Publications of the Government's analysis, assessment and research activities 4/2017. Prime Minister's Office. http://tietokayttoon.fi/documents/10616/3866814/4_Saamelaisten+oikeuksien+toteutuminen+kansainv%C3%A4linen+oikeusvertaileva+tutkimus/e765f819-d90c-4318-9ff0-cf4375e00688?version=1.0. Accessed 22 June 2017.

Inda, Jonathan Xavier, ed. 2005. *Anthropologies of Modernity. Foucault. Governmentality, and Life Politics*. Malden: Blackwell Publishing.

Joona, Tanja. 2015. The Definition of a Sami Person in Finland and Its Application. In *Indigenous Rights in Scandinavia. Autonomous Sami Law*, ed. Christina Allard and Susann Funderud Skogvang, 155–172. London: Routledge.

Joseph, Jonathan. 2013. Resilience as Embedded Neoliberalism: A Governmentality Approach. *Resilience: International Policies, Practices and Discourses* 1 (1): 38–52.

Kleist, Nauja, and Stef Jansen. 2016. Introduction: Hope over Time—Crisis, Immobility and Future-Making. *History and Anthropology* 27 (4): 373–392.

Knafla, Louis A., and Haijo Westra. 2010. *Aboriginal Title and Indigenous Peoples: Canada, Australia, and New Zealand*. Vancouver: UBC Press.

Larner, Wendy, and William Walters, eds. 2004. *Global Governmentality: Governing International Spaces*. London: Routledge.

Lemke, Thomas. 2011. Beyond Foucault: From Biopolitics to the Government of Life. In *Governmentality: Current Issues and Future Challenges*, ed. Ulrich Bröckling, Susanne Krasmann, and Thomas Lemke, 165–184. New York: Routledge.

Li, Tania Murray. 2007. *The Will to Improve: Governmentality, Development, and the Practice of Politics*. Durham: Duke University Press.

Lightfoot, Sheryl. 2012. Selective Endorsement Without Intent to Implement: Indigenous Rights and the Anglosphere. *The International Journal of Human Rights* 16 (1): 100–122.

Lindroth, Marjo, and Heidi Sinevaara-Niskanen. 2013. At the Crossroads of Autonomy and Essentialism: Indigenous Peoples in International Environmental Politics. *International Political Sociology* 7 (3): 275–293.

———. 2014. Adapt or Die? The Biopolitics of Indigeneity—From the Civilising Mission to the Need for Adaptation. *Global Society* 28 (2): 180–194.

Merlan, Francesca. 2009. Indigeneity. Global and Local. *Current Anthropology* 50 (3): 303–333.

———. 2016. Indigeneity in Australia: National and International Dimensions. Manuscript under review.

Miyazaki, Hirokazu. 2004. *The Method of Hope. Anthropology, Philosophy, and Fijian Knowledge*. Stanford: Stanford University Press.

Morgensen, Scott L. 2011. The Biopolitics of Settler Colonialism: Right Here, Right Now. *Settler Colonial Studies* 1 (1): 52–76.

Nuijten, Monique. 2004. Between Fear and Fantasy. Governmentality and the Working of Power in Mexico. *Critique of Anthropology* 24 (2): 208–230.

Ojakangas, Mika. 2005. The End of Bio-power? A Reply to My Critics. *Foucault Studies* 2: 47–53.

Povinelli, Elizabeth A. 2006. *Empire of Love. Toward a Theory of Intimacy, Genealogy, and Carnality*. Durham: Duke University Press.

———. 2011. *Economies of Abandonment: Social Belonging and Endurance in Late Liberalism*. Durham: Duke University Press.

Prozorov, Sergei. 2007. The Unrequited Love of Power: Biopolitical Investment and the Refusal of Care. *Foucault Studies* (4): 53–77.

Reid, Julian. 2006. Life Struggles. War, Discipline, and Biopolitics in the Thought of Michel Foucault. *Social Text* 24 (1): 127–152.

Rifkin, Mark. 2009. Indigenizing Agamben. Rethinking Sovereignty in Light of the "Peculiar" Status of Native Peoples. *Cultural Critique* 73: 88–124.

Scott, David. 2005. Colonial Governmentality. In *Anthropologies of Modernity. Foucault. Governmentality, and Life Politics*, ed. Javier X. Inda, 23–49. Malden: Blackwell Publishing.

Simpson, Audra. 2014. *Mohawk Interruptus. Political Life Across the Borders of Settler States*. Durham: Duke University Press.

Sissons, Jeffrey. 1997. Elimination or Exclusion? Strategic Discontinuity in the Post-Mabo Era. *Social Analysis: The International Journal of Social and Cultural Practice* 41 (2): 29–33.

Spivakovsky, Claire. 2006. Theoretical Passages and Boundaries: The Indigenous Subject, Colonialism, and Governmentality. In *Passages: Law, Aesthetics, Politics. Proceedings of the 2006 Law and Literature Association of Australia Conference*, 1–11. Melbourne: University of Melbourne Law School.

Strakosch, Elizabeth. 2015. *Neoliberal Indigenous Policy: Settler Colonialism and the 'Post-Welfare' State*. London: Palgrave Macmillan.

Sturm, Circe. 2011. *Becoming Indian: The Struggle Over Cherokee Identity in the Twenty-First Century*. Santa Fe: School for Advanced Research Press.

Sutton, Peter. 2009. *The Politics of Suffering. Indigenous Australia and the End of the Liberal Consensus*. Carlton: Melbourne University Press.

Sylvester, Christine. 2006. Bare Life as a Development/Postcolonial Problematic. *The Geographical Journal* 172 (1): 66–77.
Transforming Our World: the 2030 Agenda for Sustainable Development. 2015. http://www.un.org/ga/search/view_doc.asp?symbol=A/RES/70/1. Accessed 4 July 2017.
Valkonen, J., S. Valkonen, and T. Koivurova. 2017. Groupism and the Politics of Indigeneity: A Case Study on the Sámi Debate in Finland. *Ethnicities* 17 (4): 526–545.
Watson, Irene. 2015. *Aboriginal Peoples, Colonialism and International Law. Raw Law*. Abingdon: Routledge.
Welsh, Marc. 2013. Resilience and Responsibility: Governing Uncertainty in a Complex World. *The Geographical Journal* 180 (1): 15–26.

CHAPTER 6

Conclusions

Debunking the Myth of Progress

Looking back at the 20 years or so that indigenous peoples have been included in the work of the Arctic Council and the UN Permanent Forum, we feel that it is time to revisit the perception that global politics is making progress in its engagement with the peoples. It is worth asking whether real progress has taken place or whether that politics is still all promises: the promise of inclusion in global society has been around for nearly 40 years since the establishment of the Working Group on Indigenous Populations in 1982, yet discussion of indigenous peoples' (lack of) rights and their implementation is still a timely issue.

Within the Permanent Forum and the Arctic Council, the peoples have gained formal political access, but, at the same time, been placed in a position where they need to wait and be patient, as their rights and political positions continue to be clarified. The promise is that when all the assessments, reports and evaluations on their political, legal and social position have been completed, measures required by the states and institutions, the peoples' struggles will be more effectively supported. Inclusion is taken for granted as a principal political aim without problematizing how it became a desirable goal of politics in the first place and whose agendas it really serves.

Some might argue that the 20 years that have passed since the establishment of the UN Permanent Forum and the Arctic Council is too short time to allow a proper evaluation of how effective a measure such institutional

M. Lindroth, H. Sinevaara-Niskanen, *Global Politics and Its Violent Care for Indigeneity*,
https://doi.org/10.1007/978-3-319-60982-9_6

inclusion has been. It is true that, when compared to the length of the colonial past, the states' and global community's waking up to indigenous peoples' claims for rights and equal access has been a fairly recent development. However, in light of our critique that the peoples' claims may well be eternally stuck fast in the machinery of international institutions—structures that have always taken more time to deal with these claims—it is pertinent to probe the aspect of temporality involved in the retarding of the fulfillment of the peoples' rights. In our view, the establishment of the UN Permanent Forum, the inclusion of the peoples in the Arctic Council, the unwillingness of certain states to ratify ILO Convention No. 169 and the political games played around the adoption of the UNDRIP are all instances of procrastination. They represent processes through which colonial rule has exercised its power to define and order time; time has, and continues to be, in the hands of the colonizers.

Indigenous peoples have demanded equal rights, political access, increased awareness of their circumstances and compensation for their losses. In response, the global community has, in principle, supported their claims, deemed it necessary to include the peoples and undertake to further their legal recognition. As is generally the case in international political processes, the measures taken have been mostly non-binding and have lacked monitoring mechanisms. Given the declaratory nature of international agreements, it has been left up to the states to decide the extent to which they wish to acknowledge and commit to the actual implementation of these international instruments. Indeed, the ratification of ILO Convention No. 169 and the adoption of the UNDRIP illustrate that states have also taken advantage of this discretion when it comes to deciding and negotiating. Their equivocal commitment to these mechanisms reflects their power to set goals—social and legal equality, providing compensation or sharing political responsibility—and to determine the time horizon within which they might be reached.

In this equation, the peoples have their claims and rightful demands, while the states and global community have the authority to judge which aspirations can and will be pursued and when. Despite their political inclusion, the peoples must settle for promises and the waiting required before they are fulfilled. This pattern of promises and waiting has described the events that international politics likes to consider milestones in the development of indigenous peoples' rights. Initially, it took some 30 years for the UN to start discussing indigenous issues in earnest. After that, it took another ten years for it to establish a working group for indigenous issues, a further 20 to get a permanent forum for the peoples and nearly 30 more to finalize and adopt the UNDRIP, in 2007. Urges to be patient have been, and still are, an organic part of indigenous peoples being promised progress and its eventual realization. In the meanwhile, they are to wait.

If the inclusion of indigenous peoples in the UN Permanent Forum and the Arctic Council was intended to significantly change the peoples' position in international politics, our critical examination has revealed that no such change has occurred. There is no denying that institutionally, as reflected on organizational charts, for example, some of the promised progress has taken place. The dedicated slots for the peoples in these forums—the Permanent Forum itself and the category of Permanent Participant in the Arctic Council—are visible evidence of this. Through these slots, the peoples have gained a say in politics although, due to the role of these political arenas as experts, their voice is only consultative. Institutional inclusion has not translated into more de facto decision-making power. Clearly, however, these institutional surface reforms have strengthened the signal that international politics and its treatment of the peoples have changed for the better.

Looking beyond form to the substance of the politics in the UN and the Arctic Council relating to indigenous peoples also forces us to conclude that little has changed. The inclusion of indigenous peoples as political participants has not translated into an inclusion of indigenous agendas. The integration of the peoples' knowledge, interests and concerns remains in the offing, as evidenced by the 'very much in progress' mechanisms and measures aimed at integrating the peoples' knowledge, bringing forth their traditional worldviews and understanding their current needs. The permanency of indigenous peoples' political position in the UN and the Arctic Council has not automatically resulted in indigenous concerns being given space in policy debates. It is only within those areas that are deemed stereotypically indigenous—preserving the environment and indigenous culture—that the indigenous peoples are seen as having something to say. Community viability, local traditional practices and everyday climatic observations essentially exhaust the list of interests and knowledge perceived as relevant. Hardcore political and economic issues, such as the use of natural resources and the profits gained from it, as well as questions of land ownership and territoriality, fall outside the scope of the peoples' presumed interests and possible contributions (e.g. Martello 2008; Cameron 2012; Sinevaara-Niskanen 2015).

The dichotomy of Natives and Settlers lives on in the assignment of a separate slot to indigenous agendas. The compartmentalization and delimitation of indigenous concerns to local events, traditional ways of life and cultural practices sustained since time immemorial, communal ties and an intimate relationship with nature reproduces the exclusion of indigenous agendas from politics. The peoples are robbed of political leverage in the process. They find themselves in a position where their political presence—as permanent as it may be—does not open up all the political opportunities that their position might officially suggest. In the UN and the Arctic Council, let alone in other, less favorable, national and international political forums, it is a constant struggle for the peoples to break out of the stereotyped and romanticized Native side of dichotomy and to move their real-life demands and concerns forward onto political agendas.

All in all, has the time spent 'fixing' international politics and its attitude toward indigeneity changed anything and, if so, to whose advantage? For the global community, and states in particular, the political inclusion of indigenous peoples has eased an anxiety and colonial guilt. International politics has succeeded in covering itself against accusations of mistreatment and ignorance, in terms of not only past and current experiences, but also, and more importantly, any future developments that environmental, economic and social changes will trigger. Whatever challenges the future may pose, the global community can appeal to indigenous peoples having been involved on equal footing with others in the politics charged with addressing those challenges. For indigenous peoples, the attempt to 'fix' global politics has meant access to a seat from which to participate in and observe the course of that politics. They have gained physical access to the process in the UN and the Arctic, but the scope of their contribution has been, and continues to be, extremely restricted. The conditions on which indigeneity has been allowed to enter politics leave little room for it to appear in any other way than what the developed, Western, white structures of the colonizers recognize. The peoples' access has been granted on certain conditions: proof of historical marginalization and settling for a consultative role and a limited range of 'relevant' issues. Thus, the institutional inclusion that has been proposed as a 'fix' has been offered to the peoples on a take-it-or-leave-it basis. Given the peoples' historical position, they have had no viable option other than to go along with these surface reforms.

In our view, the commitment of global politics to invite indigenous peoples to join in and be a part of the process of allegedly aiming to improve their conditions—and the peoples' inclination to do so—does not mean that progress has taken place. As criticism drawing on feminist theory has noted, 'adding something and stirring' is not sufficient for altering and reorganizing structures that are fundamentally biased. This applies in the case of international politics and its desire to include indigenous peoples, for the machinery in which they are included is hierarchical, unequal and distorted. As long as the inclusion of indigenous peoples in international politics involves no more than participation—and thus fails to support a critical reframing of the structures to accommodate indigeneity in greater variety and the challenges this reframing may pose—there is no real progress to talk about. Until those structures are improved, the progress on record has been nothing more than acts of remorse, redemption and placation.

In the end, time is of the essence here, as regards not only the timeframe within which things might get better or be fixed but also the ability to define what a reasonable time to wait for these improvements is. In global politics, neither of these considerations has worked for the benefit of indigenous peoples. They have not been in a position to set the pace at which the political and legal developments affecting them will take place. Nor have they been in the privileged position where they could afford to wait indefinitely and rest assured that all the time spent 'making things better' will be worth it and the realization of their rights is just around the corner. Even when the peoples have exhausted their resources and hence pleaded for their rights, the position offered them has still been that of a patient claimant who must bear with the processes and settle for waiting. The political promise of progress has worked as a technique reproducing the position of the peoples as always 'in-between', waiting and 'on call'.

Indigeneity On-Demand

The selective invitation for indigenous peoples to enter global politics on the basis of their historical and current vulnerability, abilities to adapt, environmental and traditional knowledge, and their persistence is tantamount to the continuation of colonial control over indigeneity. As we have discussed in previous chapters, the indigenous subject that politics recognizes and fantasizes about is one that, although inherently vulnerable, perseveres and adapts. Indigenous peoples are treasured as stewards of the environment, as examples of successful adaptation and as embodiments of resilience. On the basis of these allegedly inherent attributes, the peoples earn their seat at the tables of international politics and gain the mandate allowing them to speak out and be experts on certain issues. On the flipside, indigeneity that oversteps the bounds of this fantasy or refuses to represent itself in accordance with it is excluded or fades from the radar of global politics. This pre-defined indigeneity in fact steers the formation of the political agendas that are considered relevant for indigenous representatives. The peoples' causes must remain in the realms of local, environmental and cultural issues and in a manner that focuses on the peoples' individual and collective efforts and capacities. What is more, even as they are granted a position to voice these concerns, indigenous peoples are charged with devising solutions for sustaining these allegedly vital indigenous realms.

Unquestionably, indigenous peoples are, and have been, vulnerable; and they do have abilities to adapt and have demonstrated their resilience. Their continuing existence, despite having been targets of colonial, assimilative and coercive measures, is solid proof of their capacity to adapt and persist. To critically engage with these characteristics of indigeneity is not to annul the peoples' track record of resilience. In probing the ways in which 'indigeneity on-demand' is constructed our interest has not been to examine the peoples' abilities and capacities per se but to reveal how international politics has exploited the construction of indigeneity for its own purposes.

The selective recognition and valorization of indigeneity has served international politics by limiting indigenous peoples' room for maneuver while enabling the political system to gain absolution. The inclusion of the peoples by dint of their expertise in environmental and local issues and their unique skills of adaptation has enabled global politics to assign the peoples a position where, in classic terms of international relations, they may engage in 'soft', but not 'hard', politics. The international political expertise ascribed to the peoples lies in the areas of social, environmental and cultural issues as these pertain to the peoples' local and communal situations. This consultative role is of little consequence in terms of money, power and security, the components of hard politics. Accordingly, selective inclusion has not posed any real political, legal or economic threat to states or global politics. On the contrary, with these constraints, allowing indigenous peoples to enter the global community has involved minimal expense. At the same time, politics has been able to improve its image, putting itself forward as progressive, attentive and equal.

More importantly, as the core message of this book indicates, this selective inclusion of indigeneity makes visible the ways in which contemporary colonialism operates by tampering with the subject itself. This biopolitical wave of colonialism, as we have called it, creates an illusion that global politics is concerned over and cares for indigeneity and its unique attributes.

By glorifying indigeneity as a prime example of environmental awareness and stewardship and celebrating its superior adaptability and resilience, politics turns its focus and attention to celebrating the innate abilities of subjects; it turns its gaze away from the conditions under which these subjects live—the conditions that have prompted the subjects' demands for rights, inclusion and recognition. By drawing on this 'indigeneity on-demand', politics subjugates indigeneity through glorification. It concerns itself with enhancing and nurturing indigeneity and its alleged capacities, not with altering or amending the social, political and legal status quo.

If one could once assume that global politics had, at least to some extent, undertaken to change unfavorable conditions and intervene in unjust treatment, the neoliberal turn has redirected this political will squarely toward improving the subject. It is now the subject that is required to make adjustments to itself in order to survive and, as the ultimate neoliberal dream suggests, to thrive no matter the conditions (e.g. Chandler and Reid 2016). The neoliberal world does not even promise that a subject can find shelter from its changing conditions; it only proffers salvation to subjects if they develop themselves, building up and harnessing their capacities. The interests of global politics and its efforts to develop those who 'lag behind' have shifted from trying to balance the world to responsibilizing subjects, insisting that the only recourse they have is themselves.

Indigenous peoples have become targets of neoliberal governing, not least due to their engagement in the machinery of global politics. Indigeneity has come to embody a subjectivity that must be endlessly extendable and malleable whether the context is the given political structures or deteriorating living conditions. As subjects with proven abilities to adapt, the peoples, who (allegedly) possess exceptional capacities that make them stand out from the rest of us, find themselves inundated by demands to maintain and develop their self-sustenance. The neoliberal mindset has been attracted in particular by the peoples' perseverance and resilience, as the parlance in the UN and Arctic politics discussed in the preceding chapters has demonstrated. The peoples are seen as those best able to cope, adapt and even prosper despite all that has happened and all that is about to happen. It is in this subject that global politics chooses to invest by offering it moral support, beautiful words, (limited) financial resources and space. The indigeneity that is perceived as worthy of investment is one that bears the responsibility of healing itself of its colonial trauma and that resigns itself to the sacrifices embedded in adaption. It is a subject that neoliberal politics can continuously manipulate (Evans and Reid 2014,

p. 30; see also Odysseos 2011) to suit its needs while resting assured that the subject will accommodate itself, as it has no other viable option. All of this amounts to indigeneity being thrown to the mercy of its subjectivity, which has now become a 'condition' that determines indigenous existence.

In its role as an exceptional subjectivity, indigeneity can even be said to represent the ultimate model for the resilient, enduring subject (Reid and Chandler 2018). In the midst of the global environmental crisis, extreme adaptability and heightened resilience have become desired and valuable currency. Indigenous peoples are made responsible for not only accommodating themselves to the given conditions but also sharing with the rest of us their superior wisdom and experience on how to cope with change. Entailed in this position as exemplars of resilience is an idea that indigenous peoples are to 'stay as they are'—to continue to live and practice their cultures on the edges of the world while observing changes and adapting to harsh conditions—for the sake of humanity at large as well as the planet. As role models of resilience, indigenous peoples must demonstrate and prove, through their lived experience, their skills in keeping their balance in the midst of change. What the expectation of resilient indigeneity suggests is that the peoples have a lived connection to the environment, that they live in areas severely impacted by climate change and that their livelihoods are, at least partially, traditional. As noted throughout this book, the expectation of such traditional local indigeneity does not necessarily match what indigenous lives are today.

Much like the institutional inclusion of indigenous peoples in international politics, the neoliberal call for resilient indigeneity functions through the endorsement of selected attributes of indigeneity. The commitment to nurture the ever-adaptive facet of indigeneity is based on stereotypical and homogenous perceptions of what indigeneity is. These deny indigenous peoples the possibility of cultural change and refuse to acknowledge their lived reality, which encompasses life in urban settings outside their traditional homelands, as well as participation in the modern labor market. The idea(l) of resilient indigeneity is a neoliberal political artifact that operates precisely by ignoring what indigeneity is, or could be, in all its variety. The construction of indigeneity as a category that is detached from the indigenous peoples works to the benefit of neoliberal politics. By choosing the traits that it finds useful and worth investing in, global politics exerts a tight grip on and continues to control the indigenous subject. While the global collaboration of indigenous peoples and the construction of the 'global indigenous' might have assisted the peoples in their political demands, the unity of the peoples that these developments exploit has enabled politics to target indigeneity as a collectivity with new techniques that govern subjects, the requirement of resilience being a prime example.

(In)Sincerely Yours

In this era of partnership and inclusion, it is easy to overlook or turn a blind eye to facets of inclusion that are less flattering to or endearing of the political machinery couched as it is in noble words and good intentions. The duplicity of politics—politics that has engaged indigenous peoples and declared that their situations are being improved—becomes obvious when the actual situations of the peoples are observed. The argument that institutional political inclusion would and could translate into genuine improvements has much less credibility when viewed through real-life examples of continuing dispossession. In this vein, we reflect on two contemporary situations that have gained global visibility. Although these cases are national, the questions around which they revolve have been and continue to be at the core of indigenous peoples' claims for their rights on the international level.

By drawing attention to these situations, we do not presume to define what the aspirations of the focal communities should and could be. Rather, we want to comment on the political mindset that leads to and maintains these states of dispossession and to illustrate how distant the ethos of 'progress' displayed in international politics is from the peoples' lived realities. Significantly, to find these examples of deprivation, one need not look any further than developed, Western, allegedly pro-human rights countries, even though it is often assumed that such countries have moved on from their subjugating practices. If these states have not been able to 'afford' to bring their actions on par with global awareness on indigenous rights, what are the chances of it happening elsewhere?

The plan to build the Dakota Access Pipeline, nearly 1900 kilometers long and extending from North Dakota to Illinois in the USA, is an example of the ways in which the colonial setting of Natives and Settlers is still strong, how indigenous exclusion prevails and to what extent the needs of some are prioritized over others. The construction of the pipeline has started and there have been protests against building it since the plans were initiated. The dispute centers on the use of natural resources, threats to living conditions and cultural meanings of the sites where the pipeline will be laid. Indigenous peoples and their supporters concerned over the potential risks of the pipeline have gathered on Standing Rock Reservation since early 2016. The peoples through whose lands and sacred sites the pipeline would be laid are fighting for their waters and waterways. The high risks that come with the pipeline, such as the potential contamination of rivers, are life-threatening for indigenous communities in the region. Notably, the pipeline plans were modified to protect the water reserves for the town of Bismarck, the population of which is predominantly white, whereas no such accommodation was made for the native Sioux tribes on the Standing Rock and Cheyenne River reservations. Those peoples' right to clean water remains unprotected (The New York Times 2017).

The suicide crisis in the Attawapiskat First Nation in Ontario, Canada, is another documentable series of events—sadly not an exception—that demonstrates the continuous neglect of indigenous peoples' historical and present needs. The community, located on James Bay, has about 2000 inhabitants that identify as Cree. For most of the year, the community is isolated and accessible only by plane. The inhabitants live in small, cramped and dilapidated houses, assigned to them by the state, and without drinkable running water. Among other hardships, they live amid high rates of unemployment; nearly non-existent healthcare services; limited educational opportunities; illegal substances (e.g. drugs and alcohol) brought to the community by outsiders; sexual, mental and physical violence; and environmental disturbances (e.g. flooding and toxins) caused by extractive industries around the community. The community has declared a state of emergency several times before, but in 2016 a number of suicide attempts prompted another emergency. A total of 11 people tried to commit suicide during a single day in a community where the suicide rate is already alarmingly high. Many were young people, some even children. Even though drugs often play a role in suicide attempts, it is not the drugs that kill but despair, as one resident stated. In response to the crisis, the Canadian government has promised financial support and improvements in infrastructure, healthcare and education (CBC News 2016; thestar.com 2016a). The natural resource extraction taking place in the proximity of the community should also have brought relief to the dire situation. Despite the promises, the community still lacks mental health services and, even more critically, adequate housing and living conditions. Living conditions in the community continue to deteriorate, as if a state of emergency were a 'normal' state of affairs in indigenous communities.

These cases reveal the insincerity of contemporary politics. The issues, challenges and problems that indigenous peoples face—despite promises, apologies and what seems like sympathy—are matters for the peoples, and the peoples only, to deal with and endure as best as they can. They are left to suffer, yet expected to persevere (Sutton 2009; Povinelli 2011). Whether the focal issues center on natural resources, construction projects or questions of health and well-being, they are made the communities' or individuals' burden. The 'fix' offered continues to be reactive in nature—a smoke screen of sort—not proactive. It is the indigenous communities who have to campaign against plans that are harmful to them and to their surroundings at large and have to try to negotiate with the powers-that-be in any given situation. It is up to the peoples to draw attention to their distress, yet despite their best attempts, states can remain deaf to their claims, as these examples above show.

Sadly, this is by no means a new setting. It is only in an extreme and visible crisis and after the peoples have exhausted their resources—and as a last-minute response, if then—that those in power agree to address the issues that have escalated into emergencies. And even at that point, as Watson (2009, p. 106) notes, politics may merely narrate a 'crisis' and respond primarily to this narration, not to its own failure, which has caused the situation in the first place. Along similar lines, Povinelli (2011, p. 144) has referred to the political will to circumvent and trivialize actual challenges and problems by chopping them up to "quasi-events" that elude any assigning of accountability or relations of cause and effect. A quasi-event, which generalizes aspects of and events in individual and social life, does not amount to much; it is "never anything huge" (Povinelli 2011, p. 144) and, as such, accountability and relations of cause and effect become non-issues.

Simpson (2016) has talked about the "eventfulness" of colonial politics that is manifest in an inclination to address indigenous issues through impressive gestures and grandstanding. These never actually address the full complexity of the issue, but rather create the appearance that actions are being taken and issues improved. While both Povinelli and Simpson talk about 'events', Povinelli's notion of quasi-events points to the denial of indigenous causes in their entirety, and Simpson's perspective on events highlights the ways in which politics deliberately pays only partial attention to these causes. The notions of quasi-events and eventfulness highlight how events become recognized as something far less than an emergency as well as how events that might actually amount to an emergency are treated.

Inspired by these notions, we describe the politics that continues to envelop indigenous dispossession as a politics of quasi-responses. Events that might succeed in raising concern are met with fragmented responses, if any; the peoples' political and social inclusion is always partial and only those aspects of their concerns are addressed that fit the particular narration of crisis by the powers-that-be. As the situation in Attawapiskat demonstrates, these quasi-responses are strongly in tune with neoliberal politics and its calculating of profits and expenses. The part of any emergency that is met with a quasi-response is the most affordable one. A reactive response to a mental health crisis by offering emergency healthcare services requires far less of a financial investment than fixing the substandard housing and living conditions of the community, conditions that have greatly contributed to the severe mental health situation in the first place (thestar.com 2016b).

The quasi-responsiveness of global politics is revealed in the case of the Dakota Access Pipeline. The UN Permanent Forum, through which indigenous peoples presumably have political leverage, has appealed to the USA to "ensure the rights of the Great Sioux Nation to participate in decision-making" (Permanent Forum on Indigenous Issues 2017, p. 8). Due to its composition and structure as a consultative body—a mandate preferred by the states when it was established—the Forum lacks any real power of decision or enforcement that would enable it to intervene. It can only recommend that the US government "initiate an investigation of alleged human rights abuses … that occurred during protests to prevent construction of the pipeline" (Permanent Forum on Indigenous Issues 2017, p. 8). Notably, in the case of the Dakota Access Pipeline, the Permanent Forum bases its appeal to the USA on the rights provided by the UNDRIP, a document that the USA initially refused to adopt altogether; even after yielding to international pressure and adopting the instrument, it has taken the view that the declaration does not change the status quo (Lightfoot 2012). Clearly, the set-up of international politics, which allegedly favors partnership between states and indigenous peoples, continues to be structured such that it ensures the primacy of states and their interests.

The insincerity of politics is also reflected in its desire to responsibilize. In Attawapiskat and elsewhere, instead of tackling the root causes of suicides, which have been linked, for example, to boarding school traumas and appalling living conditions, the easy 'fix' proffered by neoliberal politics is individualization of the problems. The overarching idea of making indigenous peoples responsible for finding solutions to their own dispossession and deprivation is apparent in their inclusion in international political institutions as well as in these two specific cases. From the meeting rooms of the UN to deteriorating local conditions, politics insists that the peoples find their solutions even when their hands have been tied institutionally, economically, culturally and socially. What is striking in the context of indigenous peoples is that the responsibilizing targets individuals and communities alike. As neoliberal politics concerns itself only with reforms and measures that it deems lucrative in terms of cost-effectiveness and profit, all responsibility for tackling the actual conditions and the dispossession inherited from the colonial system remains with indigenous individuals and communities. In Attawapiskat and elsewhere, the peoples have quite literally been left at the mercy of their worsening and decaying conditions.

What we find pertinent in this neoliberal rationality of responsibilization is the way in which it takes hold of and clings to the subject. It is up to the subject to demonstrate that its level of deprivation is adequate and, given the legal and political frameworks, that it qualifies for any measures that could alleviate that very deprivation. In terms of indigenous subjects, as we have discussed throughout this book, the requirement of providing evidence of recognizable difference, authenticity and historical dispossession actually sustains the peoples' ongoing exposure to the slowly deteriorating conditions to which the ruling system turns a blind eye. In order to be recognized as authentic and as legitimate recipients of what the system calls legal and political protection, a connection to a place and traditional practices must be shown. As a result, the peoples are required to stay put in these designated places and conditions. In effect, what seem like acts of justice and equality are in fact instances of violent care.

The quasi-responses offered to the biopolitical subject are equally driven by an interest in nurturing the capacities of the subject and demanding its active engagement. To prompt even a quasi-response in the first place, the subject must make strong declarations of its conditions. And even then, it is the subject itself that is the target of the response, not its conditions. This epitomizes the biopolitical care of indigeneity—a care that ultimately abandons indigeneity to its own devices.

Politics of Hope

In meting out recognition and care, politics relies on the subject's inclination to hope for a better future. As part of neoliberal responsibilization, the governing of the subject has come to hijack not only the capacities of the subject to survive its conditions but also, more importantly, its hopes and aspirations. Politics has turned to rely on the subject's desire for better things in a situation where politics cannot and will not provide the security and protection that it might have offered before. Fueled by the subject's hope, contemporary neoliberal politics narrates a world where it is up to individuals to have hope and to envision something better and dream that these aspirations could change the course of events, for them and for the world. Increasingly, the political rhetoric has also deployed hope as a tool for soothing subjects in the midst of the insecurities of the world and building a faith that patient hopefulness will enable subjects to thrive (e.g. Kleist and Jansen 2016).

Hope is integral to the ways in which indigenous peoples and their causes are treated in contemporary politics. As discussed earlier in this chapter, since its move away from patently coercive practices of colonialism, politics has been telling the peoples to wait for the improvements that are supposedly on their way. The idea has been that if the peoples only remain patient and engaged in political processes, internationally and nationally, their rights will be clarified and their situations resolved. By being included in political and legal processes, the only thing that the peoples have been guaranteed to gain is access to 'waiting room'. Being given a bit of hope through such inclusion has not meant, and will not mean, that the peoples' hopes will be realized or that having to wait constitutes a political setting where they are on equal footing with states. There are still those that hold the power and those that are expected to "persist in potentiality" (Povinelli 2011, p. 128)—a potentiality defined by those in power.

For subjects and politics alike, hope can exist only when the object of desire is in sight, even if distant and, at the moment, beyond one's reach. Hope requires its endpoint, its point of fulfillment. The utilization of hope as a tool for governing has also required politics to foster the assumption that there is an endpoint. In the case of indigeneity, the so-called milestones in politics and law have engendered an air of progress and functioned as events to which politics can refer as evidence of the promised progress. In light of these milestones, for a long time, it has been understandable and justifiable for the peoples to retain their position in waiting and for the ruling system to continue convincing them that progress is, indeed, in the offing. This in-betweenness of having promises in the air and being expected to wait captures the nature of indigenous peoples' involvement in international politics. For the peoples, progress has become one of those "ghostly matter[s]" (Puar 2007, p. xx)—matters that one can already sniff, something that is promised and that one can construct one's future on. The peoples' positioning in this game of hopes, promises, progress and perseverance has been driven by their institutional inclusion in international politics and all the political and legal quasi-responses provided by the ruling power.

Hope, as such, can be an empowering and enabling force (e.g. Miyazaki 2004; Appadurai 2013). It becomes problematic, however, when it is harnessed for the purposes of exercising power over those who are most in need of hope, those who might have no more than hope. As an apparatus of conducting politics, the offering of hope draws on an inexhaustible resource. The fulfillment of the hope engendered through promises can also be postponed indefinitely. Indeed, the fulfillment of hopes is always located somewhere out there, in a future horizon, a horizon that keeps receding and thus retains its grip on those who are waiting (Hage 2016). The temporal scope of hope might exceed that of affected subjects' existence; one might end up dying while hoping.

For indigenous peoples and their causes, the time set by the political and legal systems for delivering on their promises has been a long one. The peoples' positioning in the waiting rooms of politics, where they lack the authority to decide when their hopes might be realized, bears on their very existence. In the meanwhile, as the political and legal systems have deliberated how to address indigenous issues, the cultural, linguistic and political marginalization of the peoples has continued. The engendered hopes have not reversed the peoples' slow decay, as Povinelli (2011) has also pointed out. The economic, social, cultural and structural conditions under which many indigenous peoples live continue to erode. It is noteworthy here that the way in which international politics detaches indigeneity from the peoples and their lives—indigeneity constructed as a fantasized Other and imputed a uniformity globally—works for the benefit of that politics. By bypassing and trivializing the actual conditions, the celebrated milestones of global politics can continue providing false promises and hopes. The hyped institutional inclusion of indigenous peoples is one such false promise.

When reflecting on how to find the proper words to describe the biopolitical control over indigenous subjects in international politics that takes place through the well-meaning and sympathetic guise of progress, inclusion and hope, we had a chance to see a theater performance called CO2lonialNATION (2017) by the Saami Theatre of Kiruna, Sweden. The performance took up the question of truth and reconciliation processes, highlighting that there has been no seeing and hearing of the histories of the Saami people and that these should take place. With allusions to the historical and current practices of assimilation, racial hygiene and cultural genocide, the performance reflected on the (in)abilities of the colonial nation, in the end, to hear—not to mention understand—the peoples' dispossession. As the actors put it, the peoples can see the door that could potentially lead them away from their deprivation and from the long wait to be treated in an equal and just manner. Poignantly, they also noted that while the peoples see the door signaling a promise of change, they have been unable to find the handle that would allow them to open that door. In the meanwhile, they will just wait either for the handle to appear or for the door to be opened from the other side.

As the words of the theater manager, Åsa Simma (CO2lonialNATION 2017), so aptly sum up, the colonial practices that cause the peoples deprivation run deep and are ongoing:

> Whom
> How shall I begin to give thanks and
> show respect to the fact that we are alive
> On this land, my people
> Our country
> They want the essence of life
> Hauling us back and forth
> Even the last thread in this ragged
> attire is worthy to be sold
> We the property of headwinds
> Naked
> Numb
> Orphans
> But still alive

The peoples are, despite everything, still here and have no other option than to wait to be heard, finally. While contemporary politics has offered them a seat in its waiting room, time is long for those who wait. Politics is, once again, testing the peoples' ability to persist and persevere, all the while stifling their politics and chipping away at their claims. In this light, the empathetic move to include the peoples turns out to be violence through disregard—the very essence of the biopolitical wave of colonialism.

Kill Your Darlings?

As we have demonstrated throughout this book, what deserves critical attention in international politics and its treatment of indigenous peoples is the deceitful promise of progress. This promise—tantamount to a mantra—soothingly reassures that politics is doing its best and is on the right track. Repeated time and again, it works as an affirmation that inclusion means better things for the peoples and that the peoples' ability to adapt and their resilience are blessings that will relieve the world of the sins of its colonial past. The mantra also foretells a future where the peoples have the right to define the direction of their own lives and that their coping skills will be of vital importance. Driven by this refrain, global politics has drawn its attention to the adaptive, resilient and active indigeneity that is to take up the responsibility of securing its existence for the sake of itself and others. It is this struggling, yet coping, indigeneity that international politics considers worthy of its care.

Revealingly, that which is understood to be indigenous entails an assumption of one surviving on one's own. Before the term 'indigenous' was re-appropriated for the context of human beings, it was used to refer to flora and fauna characteristic of and native to a particular area (e.g. Niezen 2009). In this context, 'indigenous' referred to species' ability to thrive under the prevailing conditions without the need for outside interventions in or modifications to their conditions. Being 'indigenous', native flora and fauna were perceived as having the appropriate capacities that enable them to continue existing on their own. Now that this term and idea have traversed from the natural world to human life, similar perceptions of perseverance have come to apply to those parts of the population that assert their prior presence in certain areas. Unquestionably, indigenous flora and fauna can have distinctive and unique characteristics that enable their survival in particular conditions. However, the question worth reflecting on is: how applicable is the idea of resilience in the context of peoples whose 'indigenous' conditions have been subjected to harsh interventions and modifications?

The celebration of resilient indigeneity has been beneficial for neoliberal politics. The ability to draw on the perception of indigenous as something inherently self-reliant has worked like a dream for a politics that evades accountability and the potential 'costs' that might follow from acknowledging and assuming such responsibility. By making the peoples themselves responsible for trying to change or improve their conditions, politics has succeeded in disavowing its ultimate responsibility for the peoples' conditions while still retaining its benevolent appearance.

The shift in responsibility and the desire to include indigenous peoples have positioned them as responsible partners in neoliberal governing. Not only do they have the responsibility to change and alter their conditions, but they are required to perform the resistance that their newly gained political position supposedly allows. As Sutton (2009, p. 196) has observed, if indigenous peoples are to gain at least some of the rights that they claim, they are expected to constantly campaign for their causes: one must be a 'campaign Aboriginal'. The struggle of trying to secure one's existence is a burden placed upon the shoulders of the indigenous subject. Assigning indigenous peoples to such a reactive position, where they have to be 'on call' constantly, is also a form of power exercised over and through them. It is a position that wears down its subject and in doing so dilutes the subject's cause, creating a system where one can seemingly campaign for one's whole life without seeing any significant changes on the ground.

Most significantly, the idea of indigenous peoples as being the sole responsible campaigners for their rights reproduces the positions of Natives and Settlers, thus maintaining the colonial dichotomy. The power hierarchy entailed in this dichotomy historically meant the Settlers' rule over the Natives. While it may appear that the political maneuvers emphasizing indigenous peoples' active agency, responsibility and self-reliance signify a lessening of the rule of the Settlers, they actually represent the latest in a wave of practices to sustain the colonial power set-up. Indigenous claimants, now given the responsibility for changing their conditions, might seem to constitute a counterforce against the Settlers. Yet, if anything, the fact that the peoples' political presence has increased, allows states to shirk their responsibility. The Settlers rule by not taking responsibility for the conditions that they have created. Colonial control has succeeded in claiming still more territory, the indigenous subject, now subjugated by responsibilization.

It might be too idealistic to think that the colonial patterns that clearly continue to exist could be undone. However, if global politics even tried to break free from its colonial set-up—a change that could result in having fewer hierarchies and biases and more genuine awareness—it would have to kill its 'darlings'. By darlings we mean all those things that global politics treasures in the indigeneity it desires to include. This object of desire is a fantastic artifact—in the literal sense of the word—a wish list including the expectation of indigeneity as the peculiar Other as well as the unwavering requirement of its resilience and responsibility. One of the 'darlings' of global politics is its obsession for instrumental inclusion and the idea of this inclusion as a solution. Making real progress would mean international politics letting all of this go. Instead of seeking shelter in simple binaries, politics would need to come to terms with the complexity and variety of indigeneity. It would need to finally step out of its comfort zone, where it has not had to make any sacrifices, and to look beyond its narrow, now-polarized perspectives.

References

Appadurai, Arjun. 2013. *The Future as Cultural Fact. Essay on the Global Condition.* London: Verso.

Cameron, Emilie. 2012. Securing Indigenous Politics: A Critique of the Vulnerability and Adaptation Approach to the Human Dimensions of Climate Change in the Canadian Arctic. *Global Environmental Change* 22 (1): 103–114.

CBC News. 2016. Attawapiskat Suicide Emergency: Health Canada, Province Send in Crisis Teams. 11 April. http://www.cbc.ca/news/canada/sudbury/attawapiskat-suicide-emergency-help-1.3529750. Accessed 22 June 2017.

Chandler, David, and Julian Reid. 2016. *The Neoliberal Subject. Resilience, Adaptation and Vulnerability.* London: Rowman & Littlefield.

CO2lonialNATION. 2017. En teatral sannings- försoningskommission. Playbill of the Performance. Giron Sámi Teáhter and Rospuutto-ryhmä.

Evans, Brad, and Julian Reid. 2014. *Resilient Life. The Art of Living Dangerously.* Cambridge: Polity Press.

Hage, Ghassan. 2016. Questions Concerning a Future-Politics. *History and Anthropology* 27 (4): 465–467.

Kleist, Nauja, and Stef Jansen. 2016. Introduction: Hope over Time—Crisis, Immobility and Future-Making. *History and Anthropology* 27 (4): 373–392.

Lightfoot, Sheryl. 2012. Selective Endorsement without Intent to Implement: Indigenous Rights and the Anglosphere. *The International Journal of Human Rights* 16 (1): 100–122.

Martello, Marybeth Long. 2008. Arctic Indigenous Peoples as Representations and Representatives of Climate Change. *Social Studies of Science* 38 (3): 351–376.

Miyazaki, Hirokazu. 2004. *The Method of Hope. Anthropology, Philosophy, and Fijian Knowledge.* Stanford: Stanford University Press.

Niezen, Ronald. 2009. *The Rediscovered Self. Indigenous Identity and Cultural Justice.* Montreal: McGill Queen's University Press.

Odysseos, Louiza. 2011. Governing Dissent in the Central Kalahari Game Reserve: 'Development', Governmentality, and Subjectification Amongst Botswana's Bushmen. *Globalizations* 8 (4): 439–455.

Permanent Forum on Indigenous Issues. 2017. *Report on the Sixteenth Session.* New York: United Nations. https://undocs.org/en/E/2017/43. Accessed 4 July 2017.

Povinelli, Elizabeth A. 2011. *Economies of Abandonment: Social Belonging and Endurance in Late Liberalism.* Durham: Duke University Press.

Puar, Jasbir K. 2007. *Terrorist Assemblages. Homonationalism in Queer Times.* Durham: Duke University Press.

Reid, Julian, and David Chandler. 2018. Being in Being. *The European Legacy* 23 (1).

Simpson, Audra. 2016. Whither Settler Colonialism? *Settler Colonial Studies* 6 (4): 438–445.

Sinevaara-Niskanen, Heidi. 2015. *Setting the Stage for Arctic Development: Politics of Knowledge and the Power of Presence*. Rovaniemi: Lapland University Press.

Sutton, Peter. 2009. *The Politics of Suffering. Indigenous Australia and the End of the Liberal Consensus*. Carlton: Melbourne University Press.

The New York Times. 2017. The Conflicts Along 1,172 Miles of the Dakota Access Pipeline. 7 February. https://www.nytimes.com/interactive/2016/11/23/us/dakota-access-pipeline-protest-map.html?_r=0. Accessed 13 Mar 2017.

thestar.com. 2016a. How the Attawapiskat Suicide Crisis Unfolded. 18 April. https://www.thestar.com/news/canada/2016/04/18/how-the-attawapiskat-suicide-crisis-unfolded.html. Accessed 22 June 2017.

———. 2016b. Trudeau Announces New Funding for Indigenous Mental Health Services. https://www.thestar.com/news/canada/2016/06/13/justin-trudeau-to-meet-with-chief-of-troubled-attawapiskat-first-nation.html. Accessed 4 July 2017.

Watson, Virginia. 2009. From the 'Quiet Revolution' to 'Crisis' in Australian Indigenous Affairs. *Cultural Studies Review* 15 (1): 88–109.

Index

M. Lindroth, H. Sinevaara-Niskanen, *Global Politics and Its Violent Care for Indigeneity*,
https://doi.org/10.1007/978-3-319-60982-9

FSC
www.fsc.org
MIX
Papier | Fördert
gute Waldnutzung
FSC® C083411

Kolibri 360 GmbH
Ferdinand-Jühlke-Straße 7
99095 Erfurt, Deutschland
produktsicherheit@kolibri360.de